1,001 Helpful Tips, Facts & Hints from Consumer Reports

1,001
Helpful Tips, Facts & Hints
from Consumer Reports

THE EDITORS OF
CONSUMER REPORTS BOOKS
with Monte Florman

Consumers Union | Mount Vernon, New York

Copyright © 1989 by Consumers Union of U.S., Inc., Mount Vernon, New York 10553.
All rights reserved, including the right of reproduction in whole or in part in any form.

Library of Congress Cataloging-in-Publication Data

1,001 helpful tips, facts & hints from Consumer reports / the editors of Consumer
   Reports Books with Monte Florman.
      p.   cm.
   Rev. ed. of: Top tips from Consumer reports. c1982.
   Includes index.
   ISBN 0-89043-238-4
   1. Consumer education.   I. Florman, Monte.   II. Consumer Reports Books.   III.
Consumer reports.   IV. Top tips from Consumer reports. V. Title: 1,001 helpful
tips, facts, and hints from Consumer reports.   VI. Title: One thousand one helpful tips,
facts & hints from Consumer reports.   VII. Title: One thousand and one helpful tips,
facts & hints from Consumer reports.
TX335.A17
640.73--dc 19   89-30398
                                                                              CIP

First printing, July 1989
Manufactured in the United States of America

1,001 Helpful Tips, Facts & Hints from Consumer Reports is a Consumer Reports Book
published by Consumers Union, the nonprofit organization that publishes *Consumer
Reports*, the monthly magazine of test reports, product Ratings, and buying guidance.
Established in 1936, Consumers Union is chartered under the Not-For-Profit Corporation Law of the State of New York.

The purposes of Consumers Union, as stated in its charter, are to provide consumers
with information and counsel on consumer goods and services, to give information on
all matters relating to the expenditure of the family income, and to initiate and to
cooperate with individual and group efforts seeking to create and maintain decent living
standards.

Contents

vi   Contents

Acknowledgments

Our thanks to the following technical department staff members of Consumers Union for their review of the contents of this book:

> Thomas Deutsch
> Linda Greene
> Robert Knoll
> Geoffrey Martin
> A. Larry Seligson
> David H. Tallman
> Stephen E. Taub

And special thanks to Marvin Lipman, M.D., for his expert help.

Introduction

In 1983 Consumer Reports Books published *Top Tips from Consumer Reports: How to Do Things Better, Faster, Cheaper*. One of our most popular books, *Top Tips* was a compendium of facts, tips, and advice on a number of consumer items and services, all culled from past issues of *Consumer Reports*.

1,001 Helpful Tips, Facts & Hints from Consumer Reports is a revised and updated version of that earlier book. Although there are differences in format and organization, the basic material remains the same—practical and informative facts and buying advice on a variety of products and services for your home, your health, and your leisure time.

Today the marketplace for products and services is huge and varied; as a consumer, you need all the help you can get. Using this book, you'll find it easier to reach an informed decision on buying a used car, replacing a seat belt, or choosing the right kind of motor oil. You'll be better informed about caring for a bad back, preventing brittle nails, feeding an infant. If you cook, you'll enjoy the many tips on such subjects as cooking a turkey and buying a microwave oven; you'll also appreciate the hard facts on safety—when using appliances, handling chemicals, or doing renovations and repairs on your house.

And there's more. In these short, concise entries, you'll find out how to shop for an air conditioner, how to decide if cable

TV is worth the cost, how to save on mortgage interest. You'll get tips on using appliances efficiently, on cutting home heating costs, on choosing the right carpet. With this book you'll find out how to maintain and care for a lot of things—and save money and time in the process.

All the information, as before, comes from issues of *Consumer Reports* over the last few years. To guarantee the accuracy and currency of the information, we have had specialists from the technical department of Consumers Union review all items involving the testing of products, buying advice, and suggestions on using a product. Editors who prepared reports for the magazine in such areas as health and medicine, financial matters, and related kinds of consumer services also reviewed the material in this book. As of this writing, every item in this book reflects our current advice to consumers.

How to Use This Book

In *1,001 Helpful Tips, Facts & Hints from Consumer Reports,* we say everything we want to say on a particular topic in a page, or two pages. This is not a book that delves into a subject in depth. If you want more information on something we cover, we refer you to *Consumer Reports* magazine.

You can use this book in several different ways. If you like, read the entire book from beginning to end. Or use the handy alphabetical format and browse through it. We believe you'll find suggestions that intrigue you and ideas you'll want to try. Or use the index and go right to the subjects that interest you, such as making the perfect pancake, advice on buying a refrigerator or freezer, or help with lowering your cholesterol.

1,001 Helpful Tips, Facts & Hints from Consumer Reports is intended to provide consumers with a small education about an extremely large and diverse marketplace. We hope you find it practical, informative, and fun to read.

The Editors of Consumer Reports Books

AIR CLEANERS

If you can tolerate some chill, fresh air is still the best air cleaner. When the outside temperature is 20°F and the temperature inside is 70°F, opening a window a couple of inches costs no more than a few cents an hour in lost heat.

This doesn't mean that an air cleaning appliance is useless, however. Airborne dust causes many people to sneeze, wheeze, and have other allergic reactions. A good air cleaner, especially if it's used during sleep, can help reduce allergic reactions to dust. However, an air cleaner is no panacea. Since it removes dust particles only when they are in the air, an air cleaner won't eliminate regular dusting and vacuuming. For maximum benefit, then, dust sources in the home should be minimized first, before resorting to the use of an air cleaner.

An air cleaner can also help those allergic to mold spores. For pollen allergies, however, an air conditioner is better. Unlike dust and mold spores, pollen originates outside the house, generally in warm weather when windows are open. An air conditioner circulates air without introducing pollen.

Fan/Filter Systems. Many air cleaners use a fan to draw the air through a filter. The ability of fans to move air efficiently varies with the model you choose.

Filters vary, too. Granular materials (activated carbon and/

or silica gel) are commonly used in inexpensive air cleaners, often in quantities too small to have much of an effect.

Another type of filter is made up of a web of synthetic or glass fiber. It works like a strainer, catching particles that pass through it. This type of fibrous filter can be made more efficient by increasing its surface area—typically by folding it into pleats. A *high-efficiency particulate air filter*, or HEPA filter, pleated and made of glass fibers, is found in a number of home air cleaners. Of course, these filters must be replaced periodically.

The efficiency of a fibrous filter is increased by including fibers with an electrical charge: the *electret filter*. Many particles in the air have a weak electrical charge, especially when the air is dry. An electret filter catches small charged particles that would otherwise pass through.

Electrostatic Precipitators. An air cleaner of this design draws in air with a fan, moving it past an electrode that gives airborne particles an electrical charge. The air then passes a bank of collector plates with opposite electrical charges that trap the dust and other charged particles.

An electrostatic precipitator can be purchased as a component that can be built into a forced-air heating system (a method worth considering if you want to clean the air in an entire house). There are also room-size electrostatic precipitators about the size of (or smaller than) a room air conditioner. Precipitator cells should be washed monthly for best results.

Negative-Ion Generators. Newly designed units can be highly effective at removing smoke without emitting the toxic ozone that was a problem with some designs of a generation ago. A negative-ion generator spews electrons into the air, turning air molecules into negative ions that seem to give airborne particles a negative charge. If the unit lacks a fan and collecting filter, the particles drift to grounded surfaces such as walls and ceilings, where they stick, along with smoke particles. This method can stain walls more than other types of air cleaners do.

AIR CONDITIONERS

The first step in choosing a room air conditioner is to determine the cooling capacity you need. An undersize air conditioner won't cool adequately; an oversize unit may cycle off before it can dehumidify your room.

The smallest room air conditioners have a cooling capacity of about 4,000 British thermal units (Btu) per hour; the largest, about 20,000 Btu per hour. Estimating the cooling capacity by rules of thumb often doesn't work. To estimate properly, use the worksheet on pages 8–9 to determine which size meets your needs.

You should also look for a unit that uses the least amount of electricity. Every new air conditioner carries a tag that lists its energy efficiency ratio (EER). The higher the EER, the less the unit will cost to run. Some models have an "energy saver" setting that shuts off the fan when the compressor cycles off. However, the feature isn't likely to save much electricity—it's the compressor, not the fan, that uses most of an air conditioner's power. The setting may also make a room feel slightly stuffy.

Brownouts. In very hot weather, power companies often lower the line voltage. The low voltage may make it difficult to restart your compressor when it cycles off. If this occurs, set the air conditioner's thermostat at maximum cooling, to keep the compressor from cycling. Alternatively, turn the thermostat to a warmer setting to give the air conditioner a longer rest between cycles.

Installation. Your first step will usually be to mount a support bracket on the windowsill to brace the unit; the bracket often includes a leveling provision to ensure a slight tilt toward

WORKSHEET: HOW POWERFUL AN AIR CONDITIONER DO YOU NEED?

This worksheet, adapted from one published by the Association of Home Appliance Manufacturers, can help you estimate how much cooling capacity you need. *Note:* Consider rooms connected by a permanently open door or archway more than 5 feet wide as one large room. If the air conditioner will be used only at night, use the factors given in parentheses to calculate the cooling load.

1. Heat gain through doors. Multiply the total width of all continually open doors in the room by the factor given. Consider rooms connected by a door or archway more than 5 feet wide as one large space.

_____ ft × 300(200) = _____

2. Sun through windows. Multiply window area by the applicable factor. Multiply factor by 0.5 for any window with glass block; multiply factor by 0.8 for double glass or storm window. Enter only the largest number you calculate in the column at right. Disregard this item if air conditioner will be used only for night cooling.

Window facing	No shades		Inside shades		Outside awnings	
Northeast	_____ sq ft ×	60	or	25	or	20 =
East	_____ sq ft ×	80	or	40	or	25 =
Southeast	_____ sq ft ×	75	or	30	or	20 =
South	_____ sq ft ×	75	or	35	or	20 =
Southwest	_____ sq ft ×	110	or	45	or	30 =
West	_____ sq ft ×	150	or	65	or	45 =
Northwest	_____ sq ft ×	120	or	50	or	35 =
North	_____ sq ft ×	0	or	0	or	0 =

(Enter only largest factor)

3. Conduction through windows. Multiply total area of all windows by the factor given (use 7 as the factor if the windows have double glass or glass block).

_____ sq ft × 14 = _____

4. Heat gain from walls. Multiply total length, in feet, of all walls by the appropriate factor. Consider walls shaded by adjacent structures but not by foliage as having north exposure. "Light" means an uninsulated frame wall or a masonry wall no more than 8 inches thick. "Heavy" means insulated frame or masonry more than 8 inches thick.

	Light		Heavy	
Outside, facing north:	_____ ft × 30(30)	or	20(20)	= _____
Other outside walls:	_____ ft × 60(30)	or	30(20)	= _____
Inside walls:	_____ ft × 30(30)	or	20(20)	= _____

5. Heat gain through ceiling. Locate the type of construction that most closely matches that of the room to be cooled. Multiply the total ceiling area by the appropriate factor. Enter only one figure at far right.

Uninsulated, no space above   ____sq ft × 19(5) = ____
Uninsulated, attic above   ____sq ft × 12(7) = ____
Insulated, no space above   ____sq ft × 8(3) = ____
Insulated, attic above   ____sq ft × 5(4) = ____
Occupied space above   ____sq ft × 3(3) = ____

(Enter only one figure)

6. Heat gain through floor. Multiply total floor area by the factor given. Disregard this item if the floor is directly on the ground or over a basement.

____sq ft × 3 = ____

7. Subtotal. Add lines 1 through 6. Enter the result here.

____

8. Climate correction. Multiply the figure on line 7 by the climate-correction factor for your locality. Find the factor from the map on page 10.

____ (subtotal from line 7) × ____ (factor from map) = ____

9. Heat from people. Multiply the number of people who will occupy the room to be cooled by the factor given. Use a minimum of 2 people.

____ (number of people) × 600 = ____

10. Heat from electrical equipment. Determine the total wattage for lights and electrical equipment in the room to be cooled. Don't include the air conditioner itself. If the appliance nameplate doesn't list the wattage, multiply the amperage by the voltage for an approximation.

____ (total wattage) × 3 = ____

11. Total cooling load. Add lines 8, 9, and 10. Enter the sum here. This number tells you how many British thermal units (Btu) of heat build up in the room each hour. Therefore, you want to choose an air conditioner with a cooling capacity (Btu per hour) that will nearly match the heat buildup you've calculated. A difference of about 5 percent between the number you calculate and the air conditioner's capacity shouldn't be significant.

____

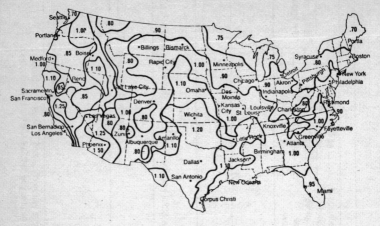

(See worksheet, pages 8–9)

the outside. With big air conditioners, a slide-out chassis is a convenience—you can mount the empty cabinet before sliding in the heavy part. Most air conditioners come with expandable curtains to fill the space at their sides. Metal frames are stronger than plastic.

Maintenance. Check the filter every week or so and wash or vacuum it as needed. A clogged filter reduces an air conditioner's effectiveness. It's also a good idea to dust the coil fins occasionally, inside and out. Some manufacturers suggest that you oil the fan motor periodically. This is easiest to do on models with a slide-out chassis.

Buy Early. Late spring is best, before summer heat waves deplete retailers' stocks and your choice becomes limited.

AIRLINE OVERBOOKING

Almost all airlines overbook—that is, they sell more tickets for a given flight than they have seats. The federal government allows the practice because up to 20 percent of all passengers who reserve seats don't show up. But you have certain rights if you're denied a seat on a flight you've paid for.

If a flight is overbooked, federal regulations require that the airline ask for volunteers who are willing to take a later flight. The airline will offer some sort of compensation, usually a coupon good for a free domestic flight. Don't volunteer unless you're given a confirmed seat on an acceptable substitute flight. If you're merely put on standby or on a waiting list, you might not get on that plane either.

If there aren't enough volunteers, the airline will systematically deny boarding to certain passengers, usually beginning with those who checked in last. If you are involuntarily bumped, you may be entitled to compensation. The amount you are compensated depends on how late you arrive at your original destination.

If you have been bumped from a flight because of overbooking and believe you have been treated unfairly, call the U.S. Department of Transportation, Office of Community and Consumer Affairs, at 202-366-2220, or write to 400 7th St. S.W., Washington, DC 20590.

ALLERGIES

The symptoms of allergies can range from annoying to life-threatening. Most allergy sufferers have hay fever or allergic rhinitis. Less common problems include asthma, skin diseases such as eczema, and food allergies.

The most effective way to treat an allergy is simply to avoid what causes it. Allergists always recommend avoidance *before* attempting any other treatment. If your cat or dog makes you wheeze, for example, no treatment can rival the beneficial effect of giving the pet away, painful as that may be. If you react to house dust, removing bedroom rugs and putting mattresses and pillows in airtight cases may ease the problem. A dehumidifier can help rid damp areas of mold, another common allergen.

When avoidance isn't possible, as with airborne pollen, the next-best solution is taking medication to relieve the symptoms. During the past 10 years, new prescription drugs with reduced side effects have enhanced allergy treatment significantly.

Shots. When drugs fall short, however, you may be a candidate for allergy shots. These shots are effective against some allergens you inhale, such as pollens, and also against allergic reactions to insect stings. Once the cause of your allergy is identified, treatment usually begins with shots once or twice a week, with each successive dose of the series containing an increasingly concentrated amount of the allergen (but not so concentrated as to provoke an allergic reaction). Eventually you will reach a maintenance dose. The process commonly takes from 4 to 6 months. After that, you will probably receive monthly injections for at least 2 years.

Allergy shots can work well, but there is always the danger of an allergic reaction. In rare cases, such reactions can be severe.

Before resorting to shots, your doctor should first determine that:

- you've had the symptoms for at least 2 years—long enough to indicate a chronic rather than a temporary problem
- the symptoms disrupt your life because of their severity and duration
- avoidance of the allergen and/or medication is ineffective
- there is evidence that shots will work against your particular allergies

AUTOMOBILE BATTERIES

When your car won't start, quite often you suspect the battery, even when something else is causing the problem.

After the battery has been checked out at a service garage with a hydrometer or a voltmeter, and after the battery connections have been checked to make sure they are secure, have the mechanic examine the starter motor, the solenoid and the ignition switches, as well as the wiring. If the battery is run down, this may have been caused by a defect in the charging system.

Battery Maintenance. Keeping a battery in good working order is simple:

- Keep the battery firmly secured so it doesn't bounce around. Vibration and shock can affect a battery's performance. But don't overtighten the hold-down assembly or you may crack the battery's case.
- Be careful when using tools and other metal objects near the battery. Don't lay a wrench, for instance, across both terminals or between the positive terminal and a metal surface. The battery could short-circuit and spray destructive acid in all directions.
- Keep lighted cigarettes, flames, and sparks away from a battery. They could ignite the gas that normally vents from the battery case and cause an explosion.
- Be sure that any electrical connections to the battery are clean and tight. Wash off corrosive deposits, using a tablespoon of baking soda dissolved in a cup of water. (Don't let any of the solution get into the battery cells.)
- Use booster cables correctly. Reversing the connections can damage the battery and the car's electrical system and may even cause an explosion. The terminals are clearly marked: + on the positive, − on the negative. Also, the positive terminal is slightly thicker than the negative one.

• Check the alternator belt regularly (ask a mechanic to show you which one it is). Replace the belt if it's cracked or frayed—a loose belt can prevent the charging system from functioning properly.

AUTOMOBILE LEASING

Leasing a car usually isn't as good a deal as owning one. True, monthly lease payments may be lower than installment-buying payments. But if you buy, you own a car worth a considerable amount of money when it's paid up. If you lease, you own nothing after the same period.

People who lease a car usually don't avoid the normal responsibilities of ownership, either. They must still pay for insurance and maintenance. Under some contracts, they will also be charged for any unusual damage the car suffers while in their possession.

There may still be some cases where leasing a car is cheaper and more convenient than buying one. If you are considering leasing a car for a certain period of time, add up *all* the costs when you do your calculations, and carefully evaluate all the advantages and disadvantages.

AUTOMOBILE MOTOR OILS

Oil is an engine's lifeblood—it seals, cools, cleanses, lubricates, and helps fight corrosion. But you must use the proper product for your car and climate. The label on the container tells what you need to know.

The Society of Automotive Engineers (SAE) sets many motor-oil standards. The letters and numbers following the letters SAE on an oil container define the oil's viscosity grade. For example, oil labeled SAE 10W-30 is a multigrade oil. The first number, 10, refers to flow properties at low temperatures (the lower the number, the thinner the oil). The second number, 30, tells the high-temperature flow properties. The W denotes an oil recommended for winter use.

Oil thins out, sometimes undesirably, as it heats up, so multigrade oils contain additives called viscosity-index improvers. These additives make a multigrade oil behave, when warm, like a relatively thick SAE 30 oil.

However, some viscosity additives can cause damaging deposits. A 10W-40 oil contains more viscosity additives than a 10W-30 oil. It's best to stay away from multigrade oils with a wide spread in numbers, such as 10W-50. Use the narrowest spread that's suitable for the climate in your area.

If the container says "Energy Conserving," the oil probably has friction modifier additives that can help improve fuel economy by a fraction of a mile per gallon.

Most oil containers also carry an API (American Petroleum Institute) symbol that refers to performance or service level. Take API Service SF/CC, for example. The S means the oil is suitable for gasoline engines. The next letter, on a scale from A to G, indicates the oil's performance level. Some oils carry a designation such as API Service CC or DD. The C means the oil is suitable for diesel engines; the performance scale (the next letter) runs from A to D. (CD is designed for more severe service than CC.)

For gasoline engines, the SF performance level is the latest and contains a complete package of additives. In cars made before the SF level was introduced, the owner's manual may recommend an earlier level, such as SE or SD. SF oils may be used—and, in fact, are preferable—in such cars.

To increase an engine's life expectancy, change its oil frequently—every three months or 3,000 miles is a good rule of thumb. If you have a choice, use a 10W-30 oil. It can give slightly better fuel economy than 10W-40 oil and, while under stress, can provide a thicker film between moving parts than most 5W-30 oils. Also, the thicker film provided by a 10W-30 oil will benefit an older engine.

Buy motor oil at the lowest price available. Discount stores sell the same oil as service stations do.

AUTOMOBILE POLISHES

Paint, not polish, is what protects a car's finish. So be careful not to polish away the car's paint when restoring a smooth finish. If your buffing cloth is picking up much color, the polish you're using contains an abrasive that's grinding away the paint. Some other tips on maintaining a car's finish:

• Wash the car thoroughly before polishing it, since most road dirt is a good deal harder than a car's finish. If you don't, you'll only grind dirt into the paint, causing small but unsightly scratches.

• Polish that has dried too long on the surface can be difficult to buff. Polish dries very quickly on a hot, dry day, so you should tackle only small sections at a time.

• To see whether a polish is holding up, observe what happens to water on the car's surface. Beads of water that form on a well-sealed surface are rounded and have a small contact area. As the polish wears away, the beads spread and flatten. When the polish is completely gone, water doesn't bead at all but merely lies in a sheet on the surface of the car.

• Although you may not need to polish a new car, you should wash it often. Bird and tree droppings, salt, tar, and even plain dirt can eventually mar the finish. Frequent washing is especially important in the summer, when high temperatures increase the damaging effects of contaminants.

AUTOMOBILE RENTALS

There are three rental-rate schedules that cover virtually all car rentals in the United States—ordinary daily rates, reduced weekend rates, and weekly rates. Whichever rate you choose, you'll probably be charged by time, not mileage. "Unlimited mileage" has become a common selling point for most car-rental agencies. A few regional and local rental companies still offer time-plus-mileage rates or offer daily rates with a specified maximum number of "free" miles.

If you are planning to rent your car in one city and drop it off in another, the cost may increase substantially. Some of the smaller companies won't allow a one-way rental, and many of the larger ones offer one-way rentals only for certain locations—and tack on a hefty surcharge.

Collision Damage Waiver. A car-rental company will usually try to pressure you to buy a collision damage waiver (CDW). The CDW acts like a miniature insurance policy, providing coverage on a day-to-day basis. Technically, however, the CDW is not insurance, and it is not regulated as such. (Insurance pays you money if a mishap occurs. The CDW prevents someone from demanding money from you.)

You may be covered for rental-car damage under your personal automobile insurance policy. The deductible may be the same as if you were driving your own car. If your own insurance provides enough coverage in this area, you can save money by turning down the CDW. Unfortunately, the coverage for damage to a rented car on some insurance policies stops at $500 or $1,000. Check your policy's provisions or ask your insurance agent before you rent a car—and be sure to take along the agent's name and telephone number when you travel, as well as the name of the insurance company and your policy number. It's also a good idea to check with your credit card companies to find out if your annual credit card fees include CDW coverage.

A CDW generally costs $9 or more a day, sometimes equaling or exceeding the cost of the car rental. One car-rental executive has said candidly that the CDW system is really used by the industry as a technique for lowering advertised rates.

Besides being overpriced, CDW coverage is incomplete. The rental contract typically contains a provision that voids any CDW benefit if the car is driven on unpaved roads, is used to tow a boat or trailer, or is driven by an unauthorized person.

Which Rental Company? Most companies differ little, so

shop for the least expensive rental you can find. Comparison shopping is easy: you can do it in a few minutes with toll-free national reservation lines. Your travel agent can also display a full range of options on a computer screen.

Don't expect second-tier companies to be necessarily cheaper than the major companies. Rates vary from month to month and from place to place, and discounts are widely available. You may qualify for a significant discount through an auto club, professional society, or other association membership.

AUTOMOBILES: BUYING A USED CAR

Performance cars, luxury models, and convertibles are expensive even when secondhand, and many are packed with trouble-prone options. Your dollar will generally go farther when you purchase a small or medium-size sedan.

If you can, buy a used car with a known history—from a trusted relative, friend, or neighbor. Be more wary with other private sellers. Ask about the car's condition and mileage, and see if the seller will let you look at repair bills. (At the least, see if the service sticker on the doorjamb shows that the car has been regularly serviced.) Find out if the car has ever been in an accident. Ask why the car is being sold; the seller may divulge a problem you'd rather not cope with. Ask if the seller is, in fact, a dealer. If that's the case, and the ad you're responding to hasn't clearly stated that fact, proceed cautiously.

If you telephone the National Highway Traffic Safety Administration's Office of Consumer Services (800-424-9393), you can find out if cars of the model year you are considering have ever been recalled. To find out if a specific car was involved, get the car's vehicle identification number (VIN), and check at a local dealer if it's GM- or Ford-made, or through the manufacturer. You can then ask the seller to show you documents indicating that the defect was fixed.

You can't really recognize a bargain unless you know what the going prices are on specific models. A good source of such information is the *N.A.D.A.* (National Automobile Dealers Association) *Used Car Guide*. You can find it at most public libraries and banks. The guide, updated monthly, gives prices for models in average shape with average mileage (about 14,000 miles a year). A cream puff will cost more, a jalopy less.

Never buy a used car without carefully checking its overall condition and performance—on the lot, on the road, and in a diagnostic center or in a trustworthy mechanic's shop.

AUTOMOBILE SEAT BELTS

If you keep a car for more than a few years, the seat belts can become worn and need replacement. The major automakers make replacement belts for any car that originally had them. The new belts may not match the car's upholstery, but they will protect the car's occupants in the event of a crash.

AUTOMOBILE SERVICE CONTRACTS

Plain logic suggests that automobile service contracts are apt to be mediocre or poor buys. Contract sellers make money only if the buyers pay more for the warranty than the cost of the claims they make. Of course, this is true of almost any insurance arrangement. Companies try to take in more in premiums than they expect to pay out in claims. But in the case of health insurance or homeowners insurance, you should accept the unfavorable odds because the consequences of a lengthy hospitalization or a tornado can be financially devastating. This is not the case if your car's transmission breaks down.

You can avoid a great many repairs—and thus much of the need for a service contract—by buying a reliable car. But even if you do purchase a defect-free model with a good maintenance record, you may be worried about an unexpected major repair bill. One alternative to a service contract is to build a separate fund to pay for such major repairs—"self-insuring," as some people call it. That way you keep your money if nothing goes wrong.

If you do opt for a service contract, make sure that you can cancel it, just in case you have second thoughts. Most contracts allow you to cancel during the first 30, 60, or 90 days and get most of your money back. After that, you can still cancel, but you will be charged for the time the contract was in effect and for any claim already made. You may also be charged an administrative fee of approximately $25.

In any case, don't allow yourself to be pressured into buying a service contract, especially when you've purchased a brand-new car. During that first year you'll get very little for your money, considering most new-car warranty provisions.

Regardless of where you shop for a service contract, insist on getting the actual contract, not just a summary. Read it carefully before signing, and make sure that the insurer is going to be around for the rest of your contract. Too many private insurers have taken the money and left the business, so find out if the auto company is backing the contract.

AUTOMOBILE WARRANTIES

Some automakers provide "secret" warranties—informal extensions of the regular car warranty—usually to cover components that have proved particularly troublesome. It is often hard to discover if these extensions apply to your car, since the carmakers usually pass the word to their field representatives or dealers while leaving car owners in the dark.

If your car is suffering from a problem that might be covered by a secret warranty, send a self-addressed envelope with 45 cents postage to the Center for Auto Safety, 2001 S St. N.W., Suite 410, Washington, DC 20009. The Center assem-

bles information about secret warranties by gathering automakers' dealer bulletins and by cataloging reports from car
owners. Describe your car and the problem you are experi-
encing, and the Center will send you specific information.

If you can't resolve the problem with the dealer's service
manager, contact the nearest factory regional office (listed in
the car owner's manual) and ask a factory representative to
help out. As a last resort, consider suing the dealer in small-
claims court.

BABY NUTRITION

For their first 6 months of life, most babies get all the nutrients they need from breast milk or formula. In fact, their digestive system isn't mature enough to handle other foods. Babies may even push food out of their mouths with their tongue, a reflex that protects them from substances they can't properly swallow or digest. Some studies suggest that introducing solids to infants younger than 6 months just adds needless calories, since the baby will be drinking the same amount of milk.

Somewhere around 4 to 6 months, babies develop the neuromuscular mechanisms they need to swallow solids. They also begin to grow too hungry to be satisfied by milk alone. But every baby is different, so starting an infant on solids should be determined by a baby's readiness, not merely by weight or age.

How to Start. Pediatricians usually recommend starting with infant cereals, which are fortified with vitamins and minerals, particularly iron, that complement the baby's diet of breast milk or formula. It's best to introduce other solid foods one at a time, at intervals of a week or so. It will then be much easier to identify any food intolerances, which might show up as loose bowel movements, rashes, or other allergic reactions.

Keep in mind that each new food presents a new taste and texture experience for the child. So offer the food in small amounts and don't worry if you're getting more on the baby than into his or her mouth. Some other feeding tips:

• Don't feed the baby straight from the original jar or storage container. Spoon what you need into a bowl, then cover the remainder and store it in the refrigerator for no more than a few days. If you use the food right from the container, bacteria from the baby's mouth can be transferred from the spoon to the jar, where they will continue to grow.

• Rarely are there significant differences in nutrition or price among commercial infant and junior foods. You may want to avoid those few products that contain added sugars or salt or modified starches. Read the labels to find out which foods contain these additives.

BACK PAIN

If you suffer from an aching back, note that 70 percent of all low back problems get better in 3 weeks or less without any medical aid, and 90 percent get better, without help, within 2 months. If you do go to a doctor soon after the pain begins, you will probably be told to take a mild painkiller and go to bed. You'll also be advised to use a firm mattress for better support or to insert a bed board between your soft mattress and the box spring.

Old-fashioned doctors may also tell you to apply heat in the form of a heating pad, hot baths, or a hot water bottle. But the latest medical word is that although mild heat may relax tense muscles and ease muscle spasms, too much heat may make the spasms worse. Excessive heat can also cause burns. If you use cold compresses or ice packs, you'll avoid such problems and decrease pain and spasm more effectively by numbing the area somewhat. Liniments and plasters don't help at all and can cause burns if used with a heating pad.

There is no fixed limit to how long to stay in bed. Doctors

used to recommend as much as 2 weeks of uninterrupted bed rest, but 2 days may be just as effective. You should get out of bed when you *can* get out, even if your back still aches a bit. Staying longer in bed won't speed your recovery.

Don't leave your bed and move to a chair. Sitting puts much more strain on an aching back than walking. Standing in one position also increases back strain.

When to See a Physician. Sometimes the pain doesn't decrease, even after bed rest. The following symptoms suggest that your pain is more than just a common backache and may require professional help:

- pain that lasts more than a week or two and worsens despite bed rest
- pain so bad that it wakes you up at night or prevents you from functioning at all
- pain that doesn't ease up when you shift your posture—especially when you lie down
- pain that shoots down a leg
- numbness or weakness of a leg or foot
- loss of control over bladder or bowel function
- pain associated with a specific physical trauma, such as a fall or an auto injury
- pain accompanied by fever, nausea or vomiting, urinary discomfort, or by general weakness or sweating

Even if you don't have any of these symptoms, you don't have to go it alone. Medical assistance is appropriate even if you're just worried about the pain. Consult a doctor, too, when back pain occurs in an elderly person or a child.

BATHROOM CLEANERS

Many bathroom cleaning products claim to kill germs. This is a meaningless claim even if it's true. Germs are everywhere, and killing them unselectively in an otherwise unsterile environment is futile. Any bacteria that a bathroom cleaner may destroy will be replaced by others in very short order.

The typical bathroom cleaner is different from an all-purpose cleaner, usually because it contains antimildew ingredients. The most effective mildew cleaner contains bleach; chlorine bleach is, in fact, the most effective mold fighter of them all.

A Word of Caution about Bleach. Bleach by itself isn't a good all-around cleaner. So you may be tempted to mix it with other products for maximum efficiency. Resist the temptation—it could prove quite hazardous. Bleach reacts almost instantly with acid to produce chlorine gas, and it reacts with ammonia and related alkaline substances to produce a combination of chlorine-containing noxious gases.

This is not to say you shouldn't use bleach in a room regularly scrubbed down with a cleaner. Just use the two separately. Make sure that you thoroughly rinse surfaces washed with bleach—something you should do anyway because unwiped bleach can mar almost any smooth surface. What little bleach remains may soak into tile grout to prevent mold from taking hold again, but not in amounts great enough to hurt you when you next use another cleaner.

BATTERIES: DRY CELL
Do the many batteries used in various gadgets confuse you? Here's a rundown on the types you're most likely to come across:

Zinc Carbon. This is an inexpensive, general-purpose battery that discharges quickly, deteriorates rapidly at high temperatures—and doesn't work well in the cold. Many have an inner zinc casing that is eaten away as the battery is used and leaks a corrosive paste.

Zinc Chloride. These batteries are usually labeled *heavy duty*.

They last longer than zinc-carbon batteries and operate over a wider temperature range.

Alkaline. These are technically called alkaline manganese batteries, and the chemicals used in them are alkaline rather than acidic. They cost 3 to 5 times as much as zinc-carbon or zinc-chloride batteries, but they last up to 10 times as long. Alkaline batteries are good for motorized toys, cassette players, and electronic flash units. They have a long shelf life and are tolerant of temperature extremes.

Nickel Cadmium. The chemical reaction that produces electricity in these batteries can be reversed (recharged) with a battery charger. Since these batteries are expensive, and you have to buy a charger, they are impractical for devices that you use only occasionally. The best candidates for their use are devices that require a lot of power and that get regular use, such as walkabout tape players. (See also Flashlights: Rechargeable.)

Button. These tiny batteries work well in low-power devices such as hearing aids, watches, cameras, and calculators with a liquid crystal display.

Lithium. Batteries that use this metal are expensive. However, they pack a lot of power in a small package and manufacturers claim they have a shelf life as long as 10 years.

Cautions in Use. Dry-cell batteries demand precautions:

- Metal can short-circuit a battery, creating enough heat to cause a burn. Don't let batteries touch anything metallic, including keys in your pocket or purse, or tools in a hardware drawer.
- Batteries can explode. Don't burn them or put them with trash to be incinerated.
- Zinc-carbon and zinc-chloride batteries keep longer if they are refrigerated.

• Keep batteries—especially small button batteries—away from children.

• Don't recharge batteries that weren't made for that purpose.

• Don't mix batteries of different types: the strong batteries will put stress on the weak ones and may cause them to leak.

• A set of batteries will produce only as much power as the weakest battery allows, so change all batteries in a device at the same time.

Batteries for a Car *(see Automobile Batteries)*

BLENDERS

A blender is the kitchen appliance of choice for making mayonnaise, pureeing soup, or mixing icy drinks. But a blender is not at all the appliance for mincing onions or whipping cream. Those jobs are best done, respectively, with a food processor and an ordinary two-beater hand mixer.

The composition of a blender's container is important. Glass is preferable to plastic. Even though glass is breakable and relatively heavy, its heft gives greater stability to a blender with a lightweight base. A plastic container may quickly become scratched and cloudy.

Containers differ slightly in shape from one brand to another and even within one company's line. Some models have an especially wide mouth that makes them a bit easier to clean, and some have a lid that permits liquid to be strained as you pour it.

You can make any blender "pulse" by turning it on and off quickly, but a separate pulse setting adds a little bit of convenience for processing food without overprocessing it—as in crumbing crackers, for example.

Blender Variations. The *classic blender* is tall and solid, made up of a glass container atop a heavy, chrome-plated base. The controls are simple to use—usually just a switch that toggles High, Low, and Off; but that's all you may need.

You can also get a *cordless blender* that's small, sleek, and quiet. Such a machine can be used on the patio or at poolside. The biggest drawback of a cordless blender is that it's apt to be less powerful than a regular blender.

If all you want to do is make milkshakes, buy a *milkshake maker*. The controls should be easy to use and the mixing shaft should be easily removable for cleaning.

The *immersion blender* is a hybrid appliance that combines blender and mixer functions. Its strong points are portability and easy storage. An immersion blender tends to be limited to only the more liquid blender tasks. With the blender attachment in place, you can whip up a decent milkshake right in the glass or in the plastic "beaker" that comes with the appliance. Or you can puree soup in the pot—if you've cut up the ingredients in small enough chunks. With a whisk attachment, you can whip cream and beat egg whites; results are likely to be better than what you would get with a blender but not quite up to what a hand mixer can do. Look for multiple speeds. The ability to match speed with the viscosity of the food helps keep the machine from making a mess; a one-speed immersion blender will almost certainly make some foods spatter badly.

BLOOD-PRESSURE MONITORS

If you have been diagnosed as having hypertension and are under a physician's care, a blood-pressure monitor is a good investment. It's a device that will help you collaborate with the doctor in your treatment. Readings taken at home tend to be quite trustworthy, if only because you don't have the anxiety many people experience in a doctor's office. (Don't use a blood-pressure monitor to diagnose yourself or anyone else, and don't let a series of normal readings persuade you to alter or stop medication without first talking to your physician.) Take your monitor along the next time you visit your doctor, to make sure you're using it correctly.

Electronic models whose cuffs inflate automatically are the simplest to operate: you put on the cuff, position it correctly, press a button, and read your pressure on the digital display. However, an electronic machine may be in error by 5 points (millimeters of mercury) or more, at least occasionally. These types of monitors are best for checking a trend over weeks or months. Electronic machines also can be in error for medical reasons, depending on the patient. If your machine makes errors frequently, return the device: it's not working properly.

As a group, *mechanical* monitors are often more accurate than the electronic units. But a mechanical blood-pressure monitor requires dexterity, good hearing (you must use a stethoscope), good eyesight (you must read a dial), some training, and a bit of practice. Otherwise you might wind up making errors greater than the monitor's inherent range of error.

BRITTLE NAILS
Weak or brittle nails are usually not a sign of disease. A common cause of the problem is frequent or prolonged exposure to water, which makes nails swell; subsequent drying makes them shrink. Repeated swell-dry cycles tend to promote the breaking and splitting at nail ends. Swimmers, cooks, homemakers, bartenders, and others whose hands are frequently exposed to water often complain of brittle nails.

Some tips for maintaining stronger nails:

• Minimize contact with water. If possible, use rubber gloves when washing dishes or performing other chores that require water.

• Avoid using nail polish removers containing acetone, which tends to dry out nails.

- Nail hardeners may offer temporary relief but have to be reapplied at regular intervals.
- Eating gelatin or taking calcium or vitamin supplements won't help.
- A diet that's severely deficient in protein or calories will weaken you and your nails, but no specific food or nutrient will strengthen nails or prevent them from breaking.

CABLE TV

Access to a quantity of TV channels is not necessarily the main reason why people sign up with a cable TV company; often the motivation is simply a matter of poor television reception. This is not to say that the availability of movie channels and extra programming does not lure many viewers to cable TV as well. It is not at all unusual to be able to receive at least 10 more channels with cable than you can with an ordinary antenna, although, outside of pay TV channels, the quality of cable TV programming varies widely.

The basic cable programs earn their income from part of the monthly fee you pay the cable company and from commercials. Pay channels, on the other hand, charge a monthly fee in addition to the basic fee but carry no advertising.

You can expect to find several kinds of cable TV programming; some cost extra and some are included as basic fare:

Pay Movies. These channels specialize in showing fairly recent full-length movies, unedited and uninterrupted by commercials. HBO is the biggest, with far more subscribers than Showtime, which shows both new and older films. Both companies air scores of movies every month, with some overlapping programming, and both offer occasional concerts and comedy specials. HBO also covers significant sports events, such as Wimbledon tennis or world championship boxing. As far as movies are concerned, if you own a videocassette re-corder you can rent three or four movies for the price of the monthly pay movie fee, or even get them free from your public library.

The Cinemax channel appeals to younger audiences. Fes-tival focuses on movies for a general audience level, with films usually rated G or PG.

Culture. These channels feature foreign films or other rep-ertory-house fare. You can also see theater, opera, music, and dance on Bravo, a pay channel. Arts & Entertainment, a basic channel, imports similar programming, including material from the British Broadcasting Corporation.

Sports. The Atlanta "superstation" WTBS, channel ESPN, and The Nashville Network are all basic channels. However, not all sports channels are basic; some charge fees.

For Children. Nickelodeon offers reruns of sitcoms and movies along with new programming featuring talk shows, cartoons, and educational game shows. The Disney Channel has a mix of original films, new features and series, and old favorites from the Disney Studios.

Music. Music Television (MTV) offers rock videos, con-certs, and related programs all day and all night. There's also country and western music from The Nashville Network and soft rock from Video Hits One (VH-1).

News and Weather. The Cable News Network (CNN) broad-casts news and features 24 hours a day, often filling gaps left by network news coverage. A spin-off service, CNN Headline News, gives you a news update every half hour. The Financial News Network (FNN) covers business news and the stock mar-ket. The Weather Channel clues you in to everything you ever wanted to know about the weather.

Special Audience. There are a number of these channels. Among them is Lifetime, which features programs on health, fitness, and fashion, and other special-interest programming.

Public Affairs. The C-SPAN station broadcasts congressional hearings, panel discussions, and press conferences and sets time aside for call-in shows with public officials and newsmakers. A number of cable systems offer "public access" channels for such things as local city council meetings and Little League games.

Home Shopping. This channel allows you to shop at home, if you are willing to take the word of the TV salesperson about the quality and "bargain" prices of the merchandise offered.

Cake Baking *(see Microwave Cake Baking)*

CALCIUM AND NUTRITION
The National Research Council sets the Recommended Dietary Allowance (RDA) of calcium for adults at 800 milligrams daily, an amount calculated to meet the nutritional needs of virtually all healthy people other than pregnant or nursing women. The U.S. Food and Drug Administration uses a broader guideline, called the U.S. Recommended Daily Allowance (U.S. RDA), which takes the needs of teen-agers and others into consideration. The U.S. RDA for calcium, which is the amount used in food labeling, is 1,000 milligrams daily.

No matter which guideline is used, however, the evidence is in that many Americans—including the overwhelming majority of women—don't get enough calcium. Roughly half of the men over age 35 and about 85 percent of women over age 20 don't obtain the RDA for the mineral.

The deficit for women is particularly worrisome because nature works against them where calcium is concerned—women generally have smaller skeletons than men, and thus lower calcium reserves. Pregnancy, childbirth, and frequent dieting can deplete these reserves further. The hormonal changes that occur at menopause cause women to lose bone seven times faster than men. Obviously, it's important for women to build up their calcium reserves before menopause occurs.

Research done since 1984 reveals that taking extra calcium after menopause has only a marginal effect in slowing bone loss (osteoporosis). The primary cause of such loss is lack of estrogen, one of two female hormones normally secreted by the premenopausal ovaries; estrogen, in fact, is essential for preserving bone in women. At menopause, which normally occurs in women between the ages of 45 and 55, the ovaries

CALCIUM-RICH FOODS

	Calcium (milligrams)	Calories
Milk, cup	291	150
Low-fat milk (1% fat), cup	300	100
Skim milk, cup	302	85
Swiss cheese, 1 oz	272	105
Muenster cheese, 1 oz	203	105
Cheddar cheese, 1 oz	204	115
Mozzarella cheese, 1 oz	147	80
American cheese, 1 oz	174	105
Low-fat yogurt, plain, cup	415	145
Low-fat yogurt, fruit, cup	345	230
Custard, baked, cup	297	305
Ice cream, vanilla, cup	176	270
Sardines, unboned, 3 oz	371	175
Canned salmon, unboned, 3 oz	167	120
Oysters, raw, 3 oz	81	57
Broccoli, medium stalk	205	50
Collards, frozen, cup	357	60
Bok choy, cup	158	20
Kale, frozen, cup	179	40
Tofu, 3 oz	109	61
Blackstrap molasses, 1 tbsp	137	43

slow their secretion of estrogen. Women then start to lose bone at an accelerated rate. The greatest rate of bone loss in a woman's lifetime occurs during the first five to seven years following menopause. Afterward, bone loss continues at a slower rate.

The most effective measure for postmenopausal women who risk excessive bone loss is estrogen replacement therapy (ERT). Estrogen therapy is not without hazard, though. In theory, it can increase the risk of high blood pressure, gallbladder disease, and blood clots. Uterine cancer used to be a problem when estrogen was used alone as therapy in postmenopausal women. Today estrogen is supplemented with a progesterone-like hormone, a combination that may cause periodic vaginal bleeding.

For a woman at high risk of bone loss, however, the benefits of estrogen replacement therapy far outweigh the risks. In addition, recent research suggests that taking extra calcium along with estrogen may allow the estrogen dose to be cut in half, further reducing any risk.

If you believe you're in a high-risk category (Caucasian, small-boned, thin, a positive family history, or a smoker), talk to your physician. If you've already reached menopause, an evaluation of your medical history will indicate whether estrogen therapy or simpler measures—perhaps calcium supplements and exercise—are right for you.

Calcium in the Diet. Roughly three-fourths of the calcium in our food supply is found in dairy products, but good sources of calcium also include canned salmon and sardines (with soft, edible bones), oysters, almonds, and various green, leafy vegetables. The calcium in dairy products is readily available to your body; milk contains vitamin D, which promotes the absorption of calcium. Spinach and Swiss chard are also rich in calcium, but they are also high in oxalates, which bind calcium and hinder its absorption from the intestine.

Calories (*see Exercise and Calories*)

CAMCORDERS

In one neat, convenient package, a camcorder gives you everything you need to shoot a scene and play it back on your TV set. For most people, though, choosing a camcorder involves a trip into unknown territory. Look for the following features when you shop for one:

- a zoom lens that provides at least a 6:1 zoom ratio
- an electronic viewfinder designed to be used with either eye
- controls that automatically adjust the white balance of the picture
- controls that let you adjust the focus and lens opening manually (the automatic controls on many camcorders aren't ideal for every situation)

The camcorder you choose should also be easy to hold, with the controls conveniently placed. Larger models may seem bulky and cumbersome at first, but they are meant to rest on a shoulder, making it easier to hold the camera steady. Small, hand-held camcorders are neither easier nor harder to use than the larger models. The small ones are certainly easier to carry about, but you exchange that convenience for possibly shakier pictures. For long takes, a tripod is useful for any camcorder, large or small.

CAMERAS

If you buy a camera, ask yourself this question: Do I need advanced equipment or just something for snapshots? A 35-millimeter single-lens reflex (SLR) camera lets the photographer see what the camera "sees" (through whichever lens is being used) and thus compose a shot precisely. With most

SLRs, you can choose from an assortment of lenses and other accessories to "build" a camera customized to your precise needs. However, an SLR may be more camera than you really need or want. If you take pictures only on vacations and special occasions, you'll probably be happier with a simpler and less costly camera. Along the same lines, if you don't necessarily want to explore the variety of interchangeable lenses available for SLRs, there's less of a reason to own one. Nevertheless, lots of people still want to have the latest and the best. If you fit that category, you will certainly want to consider an *autofocus* model.

The automatic SLRs not only focus themselves with remarkable speed and precision, they also help with loading and winding film and with setting the shutter speed and aperture. These features enable beginners to get excellent results in most situations. Most of the automated cameras can still be used manually, so that advanced photographers can retain creative control.

As for creativity in general, if you already know how to use an SLR or are willing to spare some time to learn, you can find good value in a manual-focus SLR.

For Beginners. Until fairly recently, if you wanted a simple point-and-shoot camera, you had to buy a disc or 110 model. These cameras tend to have small negatives that don't enlarge well beyond snapshot size. The newer, automated, compact 35-millimeter camera is just about as small and as easy to use as any disc or 110 camera, and with it you can get the quality inherent in the larger frame of 35-millimeter film.

A compact camera makes picture-taking easy:

• Automatic load: You drop in the film cartridge, pull some film out, and a motor threads and winds the film through. The same motor winds film after each shot and rewinds when the roll is finished.

• Automatic exposure control: This helps prevent pictures from coming out too light or too dark. A compact usually "reads" the film's sensitivity from the metallic coding on the film cartridge and adjusts the camera accordingly.

• Built-in flash: This fires when it is needed.

The limitations of these cameras concern the advanced photographer more than the snapshooter. The exposure settings, for instance, are decided by the camera, not by you—a trade of control for convenience. On the other hand, a compact 35-millimeter camera is smaller and lighter than an SLR. That counts for a lot when traveling.

CAN OPENERS

A good can opener, whether manual or electric, plain or fancy, is simple and straightforward to use and opens all kinds of cans without skipping, jamming, or rolling off track. It severs lids completely and cleanly without leaving slivers of metal behind. It works neatly: the can opener doesn't tear the paper label, jiggle the lid and cause the can's contents to splatter, or submerge the lid in the liquid in the can as the cutter progresses around it. And it can do all this on all kinds of cans, from ordinary vegetable cans to oval sardine tins. If there's a magnet, it's strong enough to support the lid of a 2-pound coffee can.

A good *electric* can opener pierces a can's lid and starts opening the can when you turn a dial, move a slide, or lower a lever. And it shuts off automatically.

The best hand-held *manual* can openers are comfortable to hold and have a cutting mechanism that's driven by gears. The can and cutter turn simultaneously with such a gear-driven cutter, resulting in a smoother operation.

A hybrid model, the *hand-held electric* can opener, supplies the opening power but lacks the countertop or cabinet-mounted electric's virtue of letting you walk away from the can as it opens. However, it does allow you to bring the opener *to* the can, a possible convenience in some situations. A hand-held electric opener should be lightweight, rechargeable, and should operate reasonably quickly.

CARPETS: WALL-TO-WALL
Some things to do *before* you go shopping for a wall-to-wall carpet:

Decide on Color. Very light or very dark colors show dirt more than medium tones do; solids show dirt more than multiple tones do.

Gather swatches and paint chips to take with you, in case the store won't let you take sample pieces of carpet home. Try to look at carpet samples in the same kind of light that you have at home.

If you are trying to match a certain shade precisely, be aware that the carpet you get may vary somewhat from the store sample because of differences in dye lots. If the match is important, try to work from the actual roll rather than from a sample.

Measure the Area to Be Carpeted. To get a rough idea of the square yardage you'll need, divide the square footage by nine. Keep that figure in mind as a multiplier when you're considering the square-yard prices. The store will send someone to your home to measure more precisely.

Don't be surprised if the yardage you are quoted is higher than the yardage you calculated. Most carpeting is 12 feet wide, so it has to be pieced when installed in large rooms and trimmed when installed in small rooms. This "waste" can add to the yardage required. Closets and doorway insets can also add yardage, as do allowances for matching pattern or pile direction.

Ask to see the installer's plan, so you know where seams

will be located. By doing this, you can satisfy yourself that you aren't buying more carpet than you need. By living with one more seam, for instance, you may be able to buy less carpet.

Determine Traffic Patterns. You can get better performance from a carpet by matching the carpet to its use.

• *Kitchen and bathroom.* To resist moisture and mildew, a carpet needs a synthetic face fiber and a fully synthetic backing. Polypropylene resists water-based stains, so it's a good choice. Use a thin, dense foam-rubber or urethane pad underneath. A kitchen carpet should also have a low, very dense pile that will keep crumbs on top so they can be vacuumed up. In the bathroom, consider a washable carpet, the kind you can cut and fit yourself.

• *Living room.* Smooth plushes or Saxonies look luxurious and give a formal feel to a room. Remember, these textures show footprints, especially in light, bright colors. For a room that gets a lot of use, check the recommendations below for the dining room and family room.

• *Dining room and family room.* For well-traveled areas where food is likely to be spilled, consider the latest nylon varieties with built-in stain resistance. Stay away from light colors that will show stains and traffic wear and tear. Textured constructions such as frieze and cut-and-loop help hide signs of use; level-loop or low cut-pile are easiest to vacuum. A dense hair-and-jute pad underneath will help the carpet to wear well.

• *Bedrooms.* Carpets of almost any construction will do where there's little traffic. Here you can indulge in light colors, deep pile, and thick padding. A carpet that is soft to the feet will be appreciated in an area where you often go barefoot, so consider fibers that have a good "hand." Conversely, if you have to scrimp on carpet, it will matter least here.

• *Stairs and halls.* For high-traffic areas, low level-loop or low, dense cut-pile carpets give the best wear. Deep pile on stairs not only won't wear as well, it can be slippery. Medium solid colors or multicolors such as tweeds or Berbers show dirt least. Use firm padding such as felted hair-and-jute; use a double layer on stairs. Foam-rubber and urethane pads can be too bouncy to use safely on stairs.

Ask about Face Weight. This is the number of ounces of pile yarn in a square yard. Architects and decorators routinely use face weight when specifying "contract" carpet for offices and other commercial buildings. The minimum they would specify for a heavily traveled lobby, for instance, is 26-ounce carpet. More luxurious carpets have a face weight of 30 to 40 ounces or more.

Although face weight and other carpet specifications are not usually revealed to the ordinary shopper on labels, the store should have the information, since a store's carpet buyer orders carpets from the mills in those terms. So ask.

Once you've settled on a carpet, make sure you know exactly what the total price includes. Find out if you have to pay extra if the installers have to move furniture, remove door saddles and floor moldings, and take up the old carpet and padding and haul it away. Stairs and other tricky installations will probably entail an extra charge.

Your written agreement with the store should include the precise name and color of the carpet, the total square yards, and such installation details as where the seams will be located.

Get the installation date in writing, too. With some stores, particularly those that hire independent installers, there can be a big delay between the day you buy the carpet and the day it's finally installed.

CAULKS: EXTERIOR
Although caulking is only part of making a house fuel-efficient, caulking up cracks in exterior masonry, siding, open

seams, and crevices is a good place to start. Some guidelines to remember when purchasing caulk:

• If you plan to paint over a caulk, use a caulk that's latex-based. It's usually more satisfactory than a "paintable" silicone caulk.

• Don't buy a clear caulk and expect it to be invisible. It may cure colorless, but it will be far from transparent. Pigmented caulk is tinted to match siding color and is likely to adhere and weather as well as its white or clear counterpart.

• Most exterior caulks come in cylindrical cartridges. Use a simple, hand-operated caulking gun to squeeze a bead of caulk out of the cartridge and a putty knife to remove any excess.

• Latex-based products clean up with water, a real convenience when putting away tools and cleaning up the work area. Other types of caulks may require a solvent.

CEREALS: READY-TO-EAT

As nature made them, cereal grains are naturally low in fat, sodium, and sugar. But this is not true of many ready-to-eat cereals. In a serving of some packaged cereals, you eat the equivalent of the amount of fat in a pat of butter, or more. In others, you get a dose of sodium rivaling that found in some salty snack foods. And in still others, half the cereal is sugar.

Cereal grains are considered "nutrient dense"—they pack a fair amount of food value for their calories. The food value includes complex carbohydrates (such as starches), fiber, B vitamins, and protein. In ready-to-eat cereals, though, the manufacturing process removes some nutrients. Manufacturers do restore the lost nutrients, sometimes to your benefit, sometimes not. And they can and do add fat, sodium, and sugar—never to your benefit.

Much of the information you need in order to make an informed choice in choosing a cereal is right on the label. And the labeling is generally accurate.

Fiber. Although fiber has become an important selling point for ready-to-eat cereals, there's no requirement that manufacturers include fiber content on their labeling, and only some do (probably because so many cereals are short on fiber). Anyway, fiber in your diet should be perceived from an overall dietary point of view, not just as a morning "dose" of cereal.

Protein. The protein in grain is good but not what nutritionists term "complete." Unlike the protein in meat or fish, cereal protein is deficient in certain essential amino acids, which are the protein's building blocks. But you needn't worry, because cereals "borrow" nutrients to complete their protein from the milk you add to your bowl.

Sugar. Manufacturers add several kinds of sugar to make cereal more palatable: table sugar (sucrose), corn syrup, and honey. The less sugar, the better, because sugar can promote cavities by providing a feast for decay-causing bacteria in the mouth. This is especially true when a sugary cereal is eaten dry, as a snack. And the added sugars, unlike the sugars you may add yourself in the form of bananas or blueberries, are "empty calories," providing no useful nutrients apart from their food energy.

Sodium. Many people with known hypertension must limit their salt intake. In addition, about 20 percent of the general population is susceptible to high blood pressure, and reducing the consumption of sodium may make a difference for them. People who want to cut down on sodium generally don't think to look in their cereal bowl. But many cereal manufacturers routinely add salt, apparently for flavor. Cereal grains themselves contain little sodium.

Calories. Cereals are fairly low in calories—usually about

110 per ounce. (A half-cup of whole milk adds 75 calories; lowfat milk, 43 calories.) That's a number fixed by the caloric value of the carbohydrate, cereal's major constituent. Some higher-fat brands, though, contain substantially more calories.

If you are counting calories, watch out for the amount of cereal you use. Cereals have various densities: a bowl that holds exactly an ounce by weight of one brand will hold 3.5 ounces of a denser cereal, thus more than tripling the calories.

CHECKING ACCOUNTS

Banks generally used to provide the same checking and saving services to all customers, no matter how large or small their balances. No more. But if you carefully shop around, you still can find some checking account bargains.

To shop for a better-than-average checking account, look over your checkbook for several months last year—say, January, May, August, and November. Figure out how many checks you usually write and what your balance typically is. Then you can realistically shop for an account in a way that will minimize bank fees.

Some of the best deals are available through smaller banks and savings institutions. The checking account checklist on the next page should help you to make comparisons.

CHILD'S SAFETY GATES

Old-fashioned accordion-style wooden gates that open to form diamond-shaped spaces with wide Vs at the top have entrapped the head or neck of several children, causing death by strangulation. (U.S. Consumer Product Safety Commission files show that accordion "safety" gates were responsible for more than 20 serious accidents, including 8 fatalities, to children between the ages of 9 months and 30 months.)

Gates of that potentially lethal design are no longer made. Unfortunately, there are still many of these gates in use and

CHECKING ACCOUNT CHECKLIST

1. Name of bank: _____

2. Covered by Federal Deposit Insurance?
   ☐ Yes   ☐ No

3. Type of checking account:
   ☐ Regular   ☐ NOW   ☐ Super-NOW

4. Interest rate paid on account balance:
   ☐ No interest
   ☐ 5¼ percent
   ☐ Other fixed percentage: _____ percent
   ☐ Split rate: _____ percent on first $_____ in account,
       _____ percent on amount above that

5. Do I have to pay fees on this account?
   ☐ No   ☐ Yes   ☐ Depends on balance kept in account

6. If fees depend on balance, how is balance calculated for this purpose?
   (Average daily balance is best.)
   ☐ Minimum balance
   ☐ Average daily balance
   ☐ Other: _____

7. When fees apply, what are they?
   ☐ Monthly maintenance charge: $_____ per month
   ☐ Fee for each check written: $_____ per check
   ☐ Other fees: _____

8. If interest is paid, on what balance is the interest calculated?
   ☐ Interest paid daily on that day's balance
   ☐ Average daily balance
   ☐ Other: _____

9. What is the charge for:
   Bouncing a check (insufficient funds): $_____
   A certified check: $_____
   Making a deposit (if any): $_____
   Using an automated teller machine: $_____
   Printing 200 checks with name and address: $_____

10. Convenience factors:
    How close is nearest branch to my home? _____

    How close is nearest branch to my office? _____

    Number of branches: _____
    Number of automated teller machines: _____
    Bank hours: _____

some are still available in many retail outlets. We strongly recommend against buying a gate of this type. If you already have one, replace it with one of the newer models that is free of head/neck entrapments. The latest gates have straight edges and either a flexible mesh screen, plastic grids, or vertical slats.

We recommend the hardware-mounted models over the pressure-mounted gates, as long as the hardware-mounted model is properly installed. But none of these gates is perfect. Active toddlers can, and do, attempt to climb over them and may be injured as a result. There's no substitute for parental supervision at all times.

CHOCOLATE BARS

Adults buy more than half of the candy sold these days, and much of that is expensive "gourmet" chocolate.

Dark chocolate is the type most prized by the chocolate connoisseur. The best is very firm, with a brittleness that makes a piece snap off cleanly when you break it. It also melts very quickly and is, at most, only moderately creamy. The taste should be slightly to moderately sweet, with a touch of sourness and bitterness as well.

Americans have traditionally preferred the lighter, sweeter taste of *milk chocolate*. In the best milk chocolate, the chocolate impact should be intense, but slightly less so than it is in dark chocolate; the milky notes should almost equal the chocolate impact. A slight sourness and slight flavors of cooked milk, caramel, or butterfat are all right; the taste of processed milk isn't. An excellent milk chocolate is also slightly lower than dark chocolate in sourness, bitterness, snap, firmness, and speed of melting, but higher in sweetness and creaminess.

Strictly speaking, *white chocolate* isn't chocolate at all. It's made from sugar, milk powder, and cocoa butter. The cocoa butter, a main ingredient, theoretically contains no chocolate flavors once it has been pressed from the chocolate liquor. However, it is possible to detect some chocolate essence in some brands; some makers actually add chocolate liquor.

The best white chocolate should be very sweet, with only the slightest sour and bitter notes. Its texture should be like that of an excellent milk chocolate; it should have only a slight-to-moderate chocolate impact and slight milk character.

Calories. The best way for a dieter to deal with chocolate is to avoid it. Chocolate, whether dark, milk, or white, is fattening—to the tune of about 150 calories per ounce.

Alkaloids. Like coffee and tea, chocolate contains caffeine. Too much caffeine, or even a little bit if you are sensitive to it, can induce unpleasant side effects. But you'd have to consume 6 to 8 ounces of dark chocolate—or at least a pound or two of milk chocolate—to get the caffeine found in one to two cups of coffee. White chocolate's caffeine content is negligible.

Two other alkaloids, theophylline and theobromine, are closely related to caffeine. (All three are known chemically as methylxanthines.) Tea contains theophylline but chocolate doesn't.

Chocolate does contain a fair measure of theobromine. However, theobromine is very weak as a stimulant of the central nervous system, so it's unlikely that most people will suffer any effects from the theobromine in a chocolate bar.

CHOCOLATE CHIP COOKIES

The chocolate chip cookie was devised by a woman named Ruth Wakefield in 1931 when she chopped a chocolate candy bar into some cookie dough. That original cookie probably qualifies as the first "gourmet" chocolate chip cookie.

Curiously, the trend today toward all sorts of premium-priced sweets (including chocolate chip cookies) coincides with a heightened concern for fitness and nutrition. For the main yield of a chocolate chip cookie (or any cookie) is calories. They're mainly carbohydrate, with slight to moderate amounts of fat and very little protein.

There are some differences between packaged supermarket cookies and those from specialty shops or homemade ones. The packaged sweets tend to use relatively inexpensive vegetable oils. Homemade or specialty-shop cookies often have butter as the shortening, and the chocolate chip variety has a lot more chips, making it higher in saturated fats; it's also a bit higher in protein.

When you're not counting calories, try this recipe for a chocolate chip cookie with a chewy interior, crunchy edges, well-blended flavor, and high chocolate impact.

The recipe makes 40 medium-size cookies.

Chocolate Chip Cookies

     2¼   cups flour
      1   level tsp baking soda
      1   level tsp salt
     ¾   cup white sugar
     ¾   cup dark-brown sugar, packed
      2   sticks (½ lb) sweet butter or margarine, at room temperature
      1   tsp vanilla extract
      2   large eggs
      1   12-oz package semisweet chocolate chips

1. Preheat the oven to 375°F.
2. Mix the flour, baking soda, and salt in a bowl and set aside.
3. Use a stand-type electric mixer to mix the two sugars briefly at low speed. Add the butter or margarine in small gobbets, mixing first at low speed and then at high. Beat the mix until it's pale, light, and very fluffy.

4. Add the vanilla at the mixer's lowest speed, then beat at high speed for a few seconds. Add the eggs, again at the lowest speed, switching to high speed for the final second or so. The eggs should be well beaten in, and the mix should look creamed, not curdled.

5. Add the flour, baking soda, and salt, one-half cup at a time, mixing at low speed for about 1 minute, then at high speed for a few seconds.

6. Scrape down the bowl's sides with a spatula, add the chocolate chips, and mix at low speed for about 10 seconds. If necessary, scrape the bowl's sides again and mix for a few more seconds.

7. Put tablespoonfuls of the mix on an ungreased cookie sheet. Bake until the cookies are pale golden brown (9 minutes in an electric oven, 10 to 11 minutes in a gas one). Remove and let the cookies cool on a rack.

CHOLESTEROL

Cholesterol, a fatty substance that is not soluble in water, is transported in the blood by protein molecules. One form of cholesterol-carrying protein, called low-density lipoprotein (LDL), seems to promote atherosclerosis (hardening of the arteries). Another form, called high-density lipoprotein (HDL), appears to protect the body against heart disease. Evidence now indicates that the amount of cholesterol carried by each type of lipoprotein is a better gauge of coronary risk than a person's total blood cholesterol level.

For example, a total cholesterol level of 240 milligrams would ordinarily be considered a greater risk than a level of 200 milligrams. However, a person with a total level of 240 milligrams that is one-fourth HDL cholesterol (60 milligrams) may have a lower risk than a person with a 200-milligram level that is one-fifth HDL (40 milligrams).

The National Cholesterol Education Program (a policy-making group of selected experts) has decided to focus on total cholesterol and LDL cholesterol, with guidelines as follows:

	Desirable	Borderline	High
Total cholesterol	200 mg/dl	200–240 mg/dl	240 mg/dl
LDL cholesterol	130 mg/dl	130–160 mg/dl	160 mg/dl

Note: mg = milligram, dl = deciliter

Studies show that women, lean people, nonsmokers, and people who exercise regularly have relatively higher HDL levels, respectively, than men, obese people, smokers, and sedentary people. A diet high in fat tends to increase both HDL and LDL, although not necessarily in the same proportions. Conversely, a low-fat diet tends to reduce both—again, not necessarily in tandem.

Diet. Both critics and advocates of dietary measures agree on one point: various types of diet may lower blood cholesterol, but no one knows for sure which diet is best.

The National Heart, Lung, and Blood Institute convened a panel that recommended the American Heart Association diet. Specifically, the diet pares fat intake to 30 percent of total calories consumed (the national average is about 40 percent) and cuts saturated fats to less than 10 percent of calories. Polyunsaturated fats are limited to 10 percent of calories, and daily cholesterol intake is held to 250 to 300 milligrams (roughly the amount in one egg). Total calories are also reduced, if necessary, to correct obesity and maintain ideal body weight.

In practical terms, following this diet means eating more fruit, vegetables, and grain products, and much less food from animal sources—especially fatty meats, dairy products, eggs, and rich baked goods. It also means favoring fish and poultry over beef, lamb, and pork, and limiting portions to roughly 4 to 6 ounces.

If you want to try the American Heart Association diet as a possible risk-reducing measure, bear in mind that it's not a self-sufficient program. Elimination of cigarette smoking, control of high blood pressure and diabetes, avoidance of a sedentary life-style and reduction of obesity should all be part of a comprehensive program to reduce the risk of coronary disease.

Measurement of blood cholesterol, including its HDL and LDL fractions, should be one part of any overall evaluation of coronary risk. Since laboratory measurements may vary, at least two separate determinations should be made before you accept an abnormal cholesterol reading as conclusive.

CLEANSER: SCOURING

Most scouring powders contain silica, a quartz dust so hard it can scratch glass, plastic, and enamel surfaces. Many new "soft" cleansers contain milder abrasives, but even the softest can do some damage. Regular use of any abrasive scouring product will gradually scratch the shiny surfaces of sinks, bathtubs, porcelain enamel, and kitchen appliances.

• Whatever product you use, remember that the effects of abrasion are cumulative. You may not scuff up a tub right away, but light scrubbing over a long period of time will eventually ruin the finish. Don't apply scourers with a heavy hand and a hard pad. Use a sponge or a soft cloth at first, and use a rougher applicator only if you can't get the cleaning effect you want.

• Cleaning products that contain chlorine bleach or acid should not be mixed with other cleansers. Chlorine bleach reacts with ammonia or acid to produce dangerous gases.

• When you are cleaning, take off jewelry or wear rubber

gloves. Scouring cleansers can dull the polish on a ring and scratch soft gems such as pearls and opals. The chlorine bleach in some products can discolor silver.

CLOCK RADIOS

Some companies have tried to make the clock radio more useful by combining it with other appliances. There is, for example, the clock/radio/telephone combo, the clock/radio/tape deck, and the clock/radio/television.

For the most part, though, people who want a clock radio want just that, without add-ons. You can buy one for as little as $10 and throw it away if it breaks. If you spend a bit more than that, you can expect to get a reliable clock, a wide selection of features, and a radio that delivers fair-to-middling tone quality.

CLOTHES DRYERS

If you're in the market for a clothes dryer, you'll be happiest with one that has a moisture sensor. A sensor directly samples the moisture of the load, and shuts the machine off when the load is dry, avoiding wasteful overdrying. The alternative, the temperature sensor, checks the load's dampness indirectly: As the clothes dry, air leaving the drum gets progressively hotter until the thermostat shuts off the heat. The timer then advances until the heat goes on again. This sort of back-and-forth action continues until the heating part of the cycle has ended.

A moisture sensor, usually found in full-featured models, adds anywhere from $25 to $40 to a dryer's price. In some major brands, however, even models lower in the line feature a moisture sensor.

Permanent Press. All fabrics—but especially permanent-press clothes—will wrinkle if left in a warm heap. It's best to remove a load from the machine as soon as it's dry. Because this is often not feasible, dryers have a tumble-without-heat phase at the end of any automatic cycle to reduce wrinkle problems.

This cool-down is generally extended to some degree when you set the machine for permanent press, the idea being to cool the load to room temperature. A short cool-down period causes some dryers to leave the load too warm. With most models, however, when you put the load in to dry, you can set an extra tumble period of 15 to 150 minutes to follow the automatic or permanent-press cycle.

Gas versus Electric. A gas dryer handles clothes about as well as an electric model, but for less than one-third the cost per load (where fuel is billed at national average rates: electricity at 8 cents per kilowatt-hour, gas at 61.7 cents per therm, which is about 100 cubic feet). Drying a 10-pound load at these rates runs about 6 cents with gas, more than three times that with electricity. This estimate includes the electricity for the gas dryer's motor and controls.

If natural gas (as opposed to LP or bottled gas) is available to you, it's worth spending the extra $40 or so that a gas dryer commands over its electric counterpart. The difference in purchase price can easily be made up in running-cost savings in the first year of use. Be sure to order a gas dryer specifically for the sort of gas (LP or whatever) it will burn.

Venting. A clothes dryer extracts lots of water from clothes in the form of warm vapor. The dryer generally needs to be vented outdoors to prevent condensation from accumulating in the room. Depending on your installation requirements, a machine may have to be vented from the rear, from the side, or from the bottom—an important consideration in some installations.

COFFEE
For many people, any cup of coffee that's hot, wet, and caffeinated will do the job of helping them wake up in the morn-

ing. But a great many relish coffee's unique taste as well as its caffeine jolt.

The two main coffee species are *Coffea robusta* and *Coffea arabica*. The robusta strain is the hardier of the two, but its taste has been described as harsh, rubbery, and even a bit like cereal. Robusta beans are often sidetracked into instant or institutional-grade coffees or are used in bargain blends. Arabica beans are reserved for the world's premium coffees. Such coffees are often identified by their geographic origins (Arabian, Brazilian, Colombian, Haitian, Hawaiian Kona, Indonesian—such as Java or, when mixed with Yemeni beans, Mocha-Java—and Kenyan).

Some tips for brewing the best:

- If you grind coffee beans just before brewing, you will get a noticeably better brew than you would get from ground coffee in a can or bag.
- Freeze all unused coffee—whether whole beans or ground—in a dry, airtight container. Otherwise, you risk losing the delicate coffee scents and flavors.
- When brewing, always use cold, fresh water—bottled, if necessary—and scrupulously clean utensils. Oils that accumulate in the coffee pot will spoil the flavor.
- Use the grind correct for your coffee maker.
- Don't stint on coffee by trying to squeeze too many cups from too little coffee. If you prefer weak coffee, it's best to make a full-strength cup and then dilute it with hot water. Using too little coffee results in overextraction and a bitter taste.
- Coffee is best prepared with water just below the boil—about 190°F. Serve it promptly, though you can keep coffee hot in a thermally insulated bottle or carafe for a few hours with little loss in quality. You can also warm it in a microwave oven with little loss in taste. But keeping coffee on a low

burner too long—or worse, reheating or boiling it—can turn the taste flat, harsh, sour, or bitter.

COFFEE AND CAFFEINE

Caffeine is present in chocolate as well as in tea, but it is present in coffee in greater amounts than in any other food.

Caffeine stimulates the central nervous system, makes the heart beat faster, speeds up metabolism, promotes secretion of stomach acid, and steps up production of urine. It also widens some blood vessels, narrows others, and increases capacity for muscular work.

As with any drug, caffeine in large doses can produce unpleasant side effects; some people are sensitive to even small amounts. The characteristic stimulant effects in a typical adult are produced by an estimated 150 to 250 milligrams of caffeine, about the amount in one or two cups of fresh-brewed coffee. Caffeinism, the chronic caffeine intoxication popularly known as "coffee nerves," typically shows up at daily intakes ranging from 200 to 750 milligrams. But, if you are sensitive to caffeine, it may take only a single cup of coffee to bring on such symptoms as restlessness, disturbed sleep, heart palpitations, stomach irritation, and diarrhea.

Caffeine is also mildly addictive. Cutting one's intake can bring on withdrawal symptoms, such as headache and depression, for a day or two.

COFFEE MAKERS

A good cup of coffee requires more than a superior grind. It also takes equipment that extracts and holds the brew at the right temperature. These days, most people use an automatic drip coffee maker, the machine that has all but eliminated the percolator.

When shopping for an automatic coffee maker, consider these key factors:

Water Reservoir. It should be easy to fill. Be wary of a reservoir with a small opening or an obstruction that would force you to take careful aim with the water. The reservoir should be removable, for flexibility in use, and it should be easy to clean. This is especially important if you don't use a coffee maker every day.

Coffee Basket. A one-piece basket is easier to work with than one that's made up of various pieces that must be assembled each time you brew a pot of coffee. A basket that slides into the brewing unit is more convenient than one that rests on the coffee carafe and must be removed before you pour.

Filter. Disposable paper filters are shaped either like a cupcake wrapper or a cone, and cost up to about a nickel apiece. There are also reusable mesh filters, including gold ones. A gold filter is something of an investment (about $25), but it is capable of providing a full-flavored brew (although it may allow some coffee sediment to pass through and it takes extra attention to clean).

Carafe. The carafe shouldn't have to be turned practically upside down to be emptied. It's helpful if the carafe is marked off in cups and is equipped with a knuckle guard to prevent burns. An insulated carafe can keep coffee drinkably warm for hours on your table.

Glass carafes have been known to break in shipping. So before you buy, be sure that it is in one piece.

Automatic Drip-stop. This feature keeps the last few drops in the coffee basket from dripping onto the hot plate when you remove the carafe.

Pause-to-pour Control. This lets you pour a cup of coffee before the machine has finished brewing. That cup is likely to be quite strong, and later cups may turn out too weak if too many early cups are poured.

Brew Strength Control. The lever that does this regulates how much of the grounds get soaked with water, which is handy if you don't like coffee particularly dark.

Clock. If you fill the reservoir and basket the night before, a built-in clock timer lets you have your coffee literally "first thing in the morning." In exchange for that convenience, you have to be willing to give up something: ground coffee that sits in the basket overnight loses freshness.

No matter what coffee maker you choose, you'll probably have to experiment with the coffee to brew that "perfect" cup. If any coffee maker, old or new, isn't producing satisfactory coffee, try a finer grind, a better grade, or a darker roast. Make sure the coffee is fresh. You might also try a more porous filter; very dense filters can reduce flavor.

COMPACT-DISC PLAYERS

A CD player produces near-flawless sound. It has almost ideal frequency response; that is, it responds uniformly to frequencies from the lowest bass to the highest treble. It has almost no audible "noise." You hear just the sound actually recorded.

There's no need to spend a lot of money on a CD player. Nearly all have the necessary features and some frills, and all sound just fine. Spend more money only if you want special features for special needs.

Compact Discs. A compact disc (CD) is very different from a long-playing record. Although a CD measures less than 5 inches in diameter, it can provide about 75 minutes of playing time. There's no wear on a CD because the pickup is a low-powered beam of laser light; so if you handle a CD with reasonable care, it can last virtually forever.

Compact discs can get scratched. If the scratches are wide enough, the laser beam pickup in a compact-disc player, which "reads" the disc, won't be able to do its job properly. The result will be music punctuated with clicks and pops, or possibly a disc that can't be played at all.

You can buy a type of polish intended to reduce the number of problems caused by slight scratches. It may even be possible to restore an unplayable disc to playable condition. Some electronic supply stores carry the products needed to recondition damaged discs.

Concrete Floor Paint (*see Painting a Concrete Floor*)

CONSUMER PRICE INDEX

The Consumer Price Index tracks major consumer purchases—houses, cars, medical care, and the like. Federal officials use it to set the increase in payments for Social Security, cost-of-living allowances, and other important government programs. But it doesn't track ordinary, frequently purchased items—a haircut, an evening at the movies, dry cleaning. People usually feel the sting of inflation more quickly in these areas.

So it isn't until some time has passed that the official measure of inflation reflects what people have known unofficially all the while.

CONTACT LENSES

Most contact lens wearers, noticing red streaks in the whites of their eyes, know it's time to remove their contact lenses. Redness in the sclera, or white part of the eye, may be caused by allergy, infection, or irritation (from dirty lenses, for example, or lenses kept in too long).

Neovascularization, on the other hand, is the growth of blood vessels from the sclera into the cornea, the transparent "window" of the eye. It's a potentially serious condition that can result from prolonged use of extended-wear contact lenses.

Corneal tissue gets its oxygen supply from the air rather than from the bloodstream. (The cornea has no blood supply of its own.) Extended-wear lenses cover the cornea for long periods of time and can cause oxygen starvation. In response, adjacent blood vessels may grow into the cornea, resulting in cloudy vision. The problem usually clears up once the condition is detected and the lenses are removed.

Neovascularization is most common in people using extended-wear lenses after cataract surgery. They may wear the lenses for years at a time, except for a few minutes every few months when the lenses are taken out for cleaning.

Wearing extended-wear lenses for cosmetic reasons, usually for two weeks at a time, poses less of a hazard. Nevertheless, the risk of neovascularization is one reason that all extended-wear lens users should have their eyes examined regularly.

COOKWARE

Today pots and pans range in style from the traditional to the modern, from the fancy to the utilitarian. But some things never change. Look for the following features when buying cookware:

Handles. The handle of any cooking utensil should be comfortable to grasp but not so short that your hand can't support the weight of the pan. A pan should also be relatively easy to maneuver with one hand (except for Dutch ovens and other two-handed pots).

In general, handles made of wood or plastic stay cooler than those made of metal. Wooden handles don't last if you use the pan in the oven or wash it in a dishwasher; plastic handles are sturdy, dishwasher-proof, and can normally withstand oven temperatures up to 350°F. A plastic or wooden handle will probably wear out before the metal pan, so the handles should be replaceable.

Lids. A pan's lid should fit snugly to seal in heat and steam. A tight-fitting lid is essential for steaming vegetables and for "waterless" cooking. A lid that allows venting helps when a pot is boiling too furiously or when you want to reduce a sauce without removing the lid.

The lid shouldn't fit into a step-shaped rim. This creates an inconvenient cranny that's hard to clean.

Materials. Cookware comes in a great variety of materials. Here are the principal ones:

Copper. If you don't cook for a living, copper is impractical despite the fact that it is one of the best conductors of heat. Copper is a soft metal, easily damaged, and it needs to be polished frequently to discourage tarnish. Copper and its oxides react chemically with acidic foods such as lemon juice, vinegar, and wine, releasing copper into the food. Copper is an essential nutrient, but too much copper in your food can cause nausea, vomiting, and diarrhea. Copper pans, therefore, must be lined with a less reactive substance, usually tin. When the tin wears through—as it will if you use the pan often—you'll have to pay to have the pan relined.

Some cookware makers use copper embedded in the bottom of a utensil to improve heat conductivity. This doesn't affect the food at all, and need not create any anxiety, except about keeping the copper looking presentable.

Aluminum. This metal conducts heat quite well, even though it provides only about half the conductivity of copper. Like copper, aluminum is a soft metal. But it's light, so aluminum can be made thick enough to resist dents. A heavy-gauge aluminum pan will distribute heat as evenly as one made of copper.

Aluminum is fairly easy to clean. Cast aluminum is thicker than sheet aluminum and more vulnerable to pitting and discoloration, but it is very durable.

Steel. Steel (not to be confused with cast iron) is not a very good conductor of heat, and rusts unless it is coated with another substance, usually porcelain. Porcelain, however, is a glasslike material and quite fragile. A porcelain-over-steel utensil is a luxury cherished by many cooks for stews, sauces, soups, and other top-of-the-stove cooking where longtime simmering is the cooking mode.

Stainless Steel. This is generally an alloy of steel, nickel, and chromium. Like steel, stainless steel conducts heat poorly. But it is durable and easy to clean.

Cast Iron. Cookware made of cast iron seems to last indefinitely. A well-seasoned skillet can pass from generation to generation, like a family heirloom. Aside from its durability, cast iron is known for the crunchy coating it imparts to fried foods and for its ability to hold heat. A covered cast-iron skillet on low heat makes a fine slow cooker. But cast iron is heavy, and the metal is brittle. It can crack if you drop it on a hard surface (if the surface doesn't break first). And you have to use a cast-iron utensil regularly or it may rust.

Combinations. By sandwiching copper or aluminum in the bottom of stainless-steel pans, manufacturers can get the best from each material. The stainless steel outside looks good and is easy to clean; the copper or aluminum inside the sandwich serves to conduct heat evenly across the bottom of the pan.

Coatings. A coating can sometimes make up for some of the metal's failings. Coating a pan also can make it more decorative, more durable, or easier to clean.

Anodizing is an electrochemical process that increases the thickness of the oxide film that forms naturally on aluminum. An anodized aluminum surface is hard, easy to clean, and resists scratches. The surface won't chip or peel, but it can be eaten away by acidic foods or strong detergents. Don't wash an anodized pan in a dishwasher.

The words *Teflon* and *nonstick* are often used interchangeably for any kind of nonstick pan. Actually, Dupont has long since replaced its Teflon coatings with more durable products—first Teflon II, then Silverstone, and later Supra. Dupont claims that Supra is twice as durable as Silverstone. But Dupont is not the only manufacturer of nonstick coatings.

T-fal makes a coating called SuperT +. A European import, Scanpan, uses a light gray nonstick coating called Greblon. Generic nonstick coatings are found mostly on cheap, thin aluminum pans.

Nonstick surfaces scratch easily, though slight scratches affect a pan's looks more than its performance. To avoid serious scratches on nonstick cookware, use plastic or wooden utensils.

Safety. Some people may think that a cast-iron cooking utensil is a health hazard because tiny amounts of iron from the utensil find their way into food. They do, but a little more iron in the diet can't hurt, particularly for women between puberty and menopause. In fact, anemia in middle-aged women may have been less common when iron cookware was in greater use.

Questions about whether aluminum pots leach unsafe amounts of aluminum into food have come up repeatedly since aluminum cookware was introduced nearly 100 years ago. A recent report alleged that there was a dramatic increase in the amount of aluminum leached into acidic food (such as tomatoes) when cooked in fluoridated water. Actually, only a trace amount of aluminum shows up in food cooked in fluoridated or distilled water—far less, in fact, than the 20 to 60 milligrams of aluminum consumed in a typical daily diet, and only a tiny fraction of the 1,000 milligrams of aluminum in a typical daily dose of several popular antacids.

As for nonstick cookware, there has been concern for years about the hazard to humans when fumes are given off by nonstick pans that overheat. Nonstick pans don't emit fumes at normal cooking temperatures, but may if they are left empty on a hot burner for several minutes. (Although there are several cases of birds dying when left in a kitchen with an overheated nonstick pan, the United States Consumer Product Safety Commission knows of no incident in which the fumes have made a person sick.)

A Basic Collection. Half a dozen pieces of well-designed cookware made from appropriate materials will see you through most recipes. There is no practical reason to buy cookware in a matching set; it makes better sense to avoid a matched array of pots and pans. If, for example, you buy a set of cookware with metal handles so you can use the skillet for broiling, you are stuck with several hot-handled saucepans.

The following list outlines the basic range-top cookware every kitchen should have:

Saucepans. You'll need a minimum of two—a 2-quart and a 3-quart pan—both with lids. Look for sturdy stainless-steel saucepans with copper or aluminum embedded in the bottom and with comfortable, plastic handles. A nonstick saucepan is optional, but handy for cooking oatmeal, puddings, or sticky sauces that can make a conventional pan hard to clean.

Frypans. You'll need a 10-inch skillet that heats very evenly and a 7- to-10-inch "gourmet" pan with a nonstick coating. As a rule, skillets have steep sides and gourmet, sauté, or omelette pans have shallow, curved sides. Steep-sided pans usually hold more and are good for frying or cooking food items in liquid. The sloped sides of a gourmet pan make it easier to slide a spatula in when turning an omelette, for example.

Like a saucepan, the skillet should be made of stainless steel with an aluminum or copper bottom. Cast aluminum is an acceptable substitute, but if the pans have an anodized aluminum surface, don't put them in a dishwasher.

Dutch Oven. A Dutch oven is used for baking, braising, and "broasting"—that is, browning the meat on top of the stove and then transferring it to the oven to bake. A Dutch oven should be made of thick aluminum or cast iron to hold the heat. The handles should be metal, and able to withstand even a hot oven.

Stockpot. Stockpots rely on the liquid in the pot to distribute heat. In a process called convection, the heated liquid rises, while the colder, slightly heavier liquid sinks. A stockpot is designed with a relatively narrow bottom and high sides so that it can distribute heat quickly and evenly without much evaporation. For this type of pot, it doesn't matter what metal you use. You can save money by buying a pot made from plain aluminum, stainless steel, or porcelain-coated steel. If you choose aluminum, make sure the bottom is thick enough to resist dents.

You may want to add a *double boiler* for cooking delicate sauces; a *large, inexpensive pot* for boiling pasta and corn; and a *cast-iron skillet* for pan broiling.

Taking Care of Cookware. Here are a few simple rules for prolonging the life of your pans:

• Always match the pan size to the burner and use the lowest possible heat for whatever dish you are cooking.

• If you overheat a metal pan, don't plunge it into cold water. And don't heat a pan you just took from the freezer. Subjecting a pan to temperature extremes can "craze" a porcelain surface and cause metal to warp.

• Don't chop or slice anything in a pan. Scratches can mar a pan's looks and make it difficult to clean. Always use plastic or wooden utensils with nonstick pans.

• When cleaning, soak before you scrub. And never scour stainless steel with abrasive cleansers.

COOLER CHESTS

For a once- or twice-a-summer outing, a cheap chest can do very well. Consider a foamed-plastic cooler chest—lightweight and inexpensive, but fragile. But if you are part of a family of picnickers, it's probably better to invest in something more substantial. You may then want a "clad" cooler with a plastic or metal shell around its insulation—durable but often quite heavy.

Any chest can be made more effective with a little planning. Here are some tips:

• A block of ice melts more slowly than ice cubes. You can make your own blocks by freezing milk cartons of water. Or you can buy sealed, reusable containers of liquid that can be frozen for use in picnic chests.

• A chest packed with cold foods and beverages will stay cool longer than one filled with room-temperature items.

• Keep the chest away from heat sources; if direct sunlight can't be avoided, drape a blanket over the chest.

• Open the cover as little as possible and close it quickly.

COTTAGE CHEESE

In the days when many families kept their own cow, cottage cheese was just that—a cheese made in the kitchen of a farm cottage. The simplest version of cottage cheese on the market today is "dry-curd" cheese, which contains less than .5 percent milkfat. "Low-fat" cottage cheese contains up to 2 percent milkfat, while "creamed" cottage cheese contains at least 4 percent milkfat.

Most commercial cottage cheeses today use some sort of milk or milk product—whole, skimmed, partly skimmed, cream, or a combination. Any other ingredients, such as salt and thickeners, must be listed on the label.

The milk must be coagulated with rennet or another co-agulating substance from a federally approved list. The cheese's ingredients list will note "enzymes" if a milk-clotting enzyme was used, or will indicate "cultured milk" if a bacterial culture was used. If acid was used to set the milk, the words to look for are "directly set" or "curd set by direct acidification." The choice of setting agent doesn't seem to affect flavor to any noticeable degree.

Beyond these differences, cottage cheeses vary only in the

size of their curds. The "small-curd" variety contains lumps about the size of a corn kernel, "large curd" is twice that size, and "chunky" larger still. Curd size is a matter of individual taste.

Like most dairy products, cottage cheese is highly perishable. It isn't economical to ship it over long distances, so the cheese is generally made in local dairies.

Nutrition. Cottage cheese is a reasonable protein substitute for meat. The protein in a 4-ounce portion, generally about 14 grams, provides about one-quarter of an adult's recommended daily intake (44 to 65 grams).

Furthermore, the cheese delivers its protein without the load of calories found in meat. Creamed cottage cheese averages about 108 calories per half-cup serving—half the calories in a cooked hamburger patty, some two-thirds of the calories in a typical serving of tuna. Low-fat cottage cheese is only slightly lower in calories than the creamed type, ranging from about 75 to 85 calories per serving in 1-percent-fat cheese, to 85 to 110 calories in 2-percent-fat cheese.

You also get more calcium in cottage cheese than you do in most fish or red meat. On the average, cottage cheese provides a respectable 74 milligrams of calcium in a half-cup portion. However, a typical serving of tuna or cooked hamburger supplies more of certain important nutrients. One should include bread or crackers, fruit, or a vegetable with cottage cheese to make a well-balanced meal.

Here is a recipe for a relatively low-calorie cheesecake that can provide a tasty finish to a dinner.

Make this cake in a 9-inch spring-form cake pan and cut it into 10 pieces, each of which will weigh about 4 ounces and contain 190 calories. If this doesn't sound very "low-calorie," consider that the same *weight* of commercial cheesecake has **340 calories.**

Low-Calorie Cheesecake

1	tsp butter or margarine
2	tbsp bread crumbs
3½	cups cottage cheese (4% milkfat)
½	cup cornstarch
½	cup + 2 tbsp sugar
2	tsp vanilla
1	tbsp grated lemon rind
4	large eggs, separated

1. While the oven is preheating to 350°F, lightly butter the sides and bottom of a 9-inch spring-form cake pan. Press the bread crumbs smoothly over the butter or margarine on the bottom of the pan to line it. Beat the cottage cheese, cornstarch, ½ cup sugar, vanilla, lemon rind, and the egg yolks with an electric mixer until smooth.

2. Clean the mixer's beaters carefully and completely, and beat the egg whites in a separate, medium-size bowl until soft peaks form. Add the 2 tablespoons of sugar, a spoonful at a time. Continue beating until the mixture is stiff, but not dry.

3. Fold the egg-white foam into the batter in your first bowl. Then pour the batter into the cake pan and bake for 55 minutes.

4. Turn the oven off, but leave the cake in the oven to cool for another hour. Take it out and put it on a cake rack to cool further; don't chill it.

CREDIT CARD LIMITS

Banks today don't wait for their charge card customers to ask for more credit. They simply increase the credit limit for those with good payment records. There's another side to this coin, however. Whenever you apply for credit, the lender runs a credit check and considers the amount of your credit limit. You may be prevented from obtaining the loan you want because the lender has determined that you can't handle any additional credit, even though you don't use your credit card to the limit.

DEHUMIDIFIERS

Tired of fighting persistent dampness in your home? You might turn to an air conditioner or a dehumidifier. Both machines condense airborne moisture by passing it over refrigerated coils. But the air conditioner dumps heat and moisture outdoors and returns cool, dry air to the room. The dehumidifier just catches the moisture in a container; there's no cooling effect (in fact, a dehumidifier heats the area a little bit).

Inside a dehumidifier, a fan moves warm, humid air past two sets of coils. One set of coils is cold; moisture from the air condenses there and drips down into a water container (or to a drain). The air continues past a second set of coils (the condenser coils), which are warm. Warm, dry air is then blown out into the room.

Capacity. A critical feature of a dehumidifier is its capacity: the number of pints of water a unit can remove from the air in 24 hours. High capacity is preferable to low capacity, even if the space to be dehumidified is not very large. For one thing, a high-capacity model works more efficiently—it can extract a pint of water with less energy than a small-capacity model can. For another, a high-capacity model can handle really muggy weather, while a low-capacity model might be wholly inadequate for the job.

Water Disposal. Water drips from the cold condenser coils and collects in a plastic container inside the dehumidifier. When the container is full, the machine cycles off to prevent overflow; a signal light goes on, prompting you to empty the container. A container should be easy to position properly and easy to remove, since you may have to empty it more than once a day, depending on the weather. The odds of avoiding spills when carrying a water-filled container are better if the container has a smallish top opening—and a carrying handle.

Some models have a built-in feature to stop the dehumidifier from running while you empty the container; with the container out, the unit stops working. This helps prevent a puddle of water from accumulating on the floor.

Maintenance. To get peak performance from a dehumidifier, vacuum clean or dust the coils at least once a year. A few models have an air filter to protect the coils from dust; the filter needs occasional cleaning to be effective. A drop of oil on the fan-motor bearings once a year is also helpful.

Periodic cleanings with a brush or sponge will reduce the levels of bacteria and mold on the container's interior. (Adding a bit of chlorine bleach to the wash water may be a good idea.)

Economy. The yearly cost of running a dehumidifier depends partly on your climate, partly on the unit's capacity, partly on its energy efficiency (the amount of energy used to extract a pint of water from the air), and partly on your electricity costs. If you live in the steamy Gulf Coast states, you might well operate a dehumidifier 120 days of the year and pay $140 a year to run it, based on the national average of 8 cents charged per kilowatt-hour. On the Pacific Coast and in New England and the Plains states, where muggy weather isn't so persistent, the cost might be only one-fourth as much.

DENTAL X RAYS

A set of full-mouth X rays exposes you to nearly the suggested yearly maximum radiation dose for the face and jaws. For this reason, full-mouth X rays are needed only once every 5 to 7 years to assess the overall health of adults' teeth and gums.

The two to four X rays used to detect hidden tooth decay (bite-wing X rays) involve much less radiation exposure than full-mouth X rays.

Dentrifrices (see Toothpastes)

Detergents for Dishwashers (see Dishwasher Detergents)

Detergents for Laundry (see Laundry Detergents)

DIAPERS: CLOTH

Diaper services are still around. In fact, about 25 percent of new parents use a diaper service, which picks up soiled cloth diapers and delivers fresh ones each week. Diaper services are a convenient and economical alternative to disposables, since services charge approximately 7 to 11 cents per diaper, compared with about 13 to 31 cents each for disposables. This is a difference that can add up to $12 to $50 each month, assuming that a baby uses 7 diapers a day. Unfortunately, if you decide you would prefer a diaper service, you may not have access to one. There are only about 200 nationwide, with most in urban or suburban areas.

DIAPERS: DISPOSABLE

In the years since they were introduced, disposable diapers have continued to be constructed according to the same basic design. A disposable diaper generally has a waterproof plastic outer layer, a center layer of absorbent padding, and an inner liner that keeps wet padding from touching the baby.

Manufacturers have regularly improved on this basic design: Diaper pins have been replaced by adhesive-tape fasteners, and a form-fitting shape and elastic around the legs allow a more leakproof fit. And some diapers have elastic at the waist or extra strips of plastic to prevent leakage when the baby is lying down.

The latest technological advance is the thin, highly absorbent diaper. You can get a thinly padded diaper that absorbs up to 80 times its weight in liquid because of special crystals embedded in the padding. The crystals form a gel when wet, preventing urine from contacting the skin.

Some people have been concerned because the synthetic absorbent material is the same one used in ultra-absorbent tampons—the tampons suspected of causing toxic shock syndrome (TSS). The concerns are without foundation, however. Investigations by the U.S. Centers for Disease Control, the Consumer Product Safety Commission, the U.S. Food and Drug Administration, and state agencies found no link between ultra-absorbent diapers and TSS. TSS bacteria thrive inside the body, away from the air, and diapers are worn externally.

If there is any problem with these modern diapers, it is that they work so well that parents may change a baby too infrequently, causing diaper rash.

DISHWASHER DETERGENTS

You can save money and detergent if you have a good dishwasher and soft water, particularly if you rinse the dishes before stacking them in the machine. If this describes your situation, buy the cheapest dishwasher detergent you can find; a brand name on sale can cost less than a supermarket's own brand. However, with hard water, a so-so machine, or other dishwashing problems, it's best to use the most effective detergent possible.

Powdered detergents have been standard for a long time, even though they are imperfect. They can cake up in the box or in a dishwasher's dispenser cup. Or they may leave gritty deposits of undissolved detergent on dishes and glassware. This is more likely to happen if you pour the detergent into the machine and don't start the dishwasher immediately, thereby permitting the detergent powder to pick up moisture, which diminishes its solubility.

Liquid dishwasher detergents, relatively new to the marketplace, are supposed to solve the problems of the powdered products. These detergents are actually gels that contain a lot of fine, powdered clay and other suspended solids. They're thick enough to stay put in the dispenser cup when you close the dishwasher door. Despite the new form, liquid products resemble powders quite closely in makeup. In troublesome situations, the best performer is still apt to be a powder.

In general, a name-brand product cleans better than a store brand and is less likely to leave glass plates and tumblers cloudy or spotted. The liquids aren't as good as the best powders at keeping glasses free of water spots and food debris. And liquids can leave an unsightly film on glasses, instead of the powders' annoying grit.

Some dishwashing detergents can harm the decoration on fine china. Overglaze (the colored, somewhat dull decoration on china) is applied after the main glaze. It's fired at a lower temperature than the main glaze and thus is less durable. The same is true of gilding and other metallic decorations. We recommend that you hand-wash your fine china.

DISHWASHERS

The more expensive the dishwasher, the greater the number of buttons and cycles. As you go down a manufacturer's line, you are offered progressively fewer cycles and control options as the models become less expensive. Basic models may have only one cycle, a dial, and a switch for no-heat drying. But this doesn't mean the machine won't wash dishes well enough to suit you, particularly if you're in the habit of running dishes under the sink tap before stowing them in the machine.

Running a dishwasher takes about one-half to 1 kilowatt-hour (kwh) of electricity per cycle—about 5 to 9 cents, based on the national average rate of 8 cents charged per kwh, or less than $30 a year. Most of a dishwasher's running costs are not due to electricity, but to heating its water. The higher the water heater's temperature setting, the more it costs to heat a tankful of water and keep it hot. If you reduce a hot-water storage tank's temperature from 140°F to 120°F, you can save about $35 a year with an electric heater, and $12 a year with gas.

Unfortunately, you may not get the dishes clean with 120°F water unless the dishwasher has a built-in booster heater. Dishwashers need 140°F water to liquefy some fatty soils and to dissolve detergent completely.

Safety. Dishwashers have a built-in interlock mechanism that turns the machine off when you open the door; a sensor also guards against an overfill if the timer sticks or is tampered with in the middle of a cycle.

Don't try to clean a filter or retrieve items from the bottom of a dishwasher's tub until the heating element under the lower rack has had a chance to cool off. Keep children away from a running machine: door vents may emit hot steam.

Construction. A stainless-steel interior protects against internal scratches and chips that can expose underlying metal to corrosion. The solid plastic tub in some models should do as well. A porcelain coating resists scratches very well, but it can be chipped by impact.

Plastic-tub machines and some with a porcelain tub use a plastic panel for the door's inner surface. This is a good material for an area otherwise likely to be damaged by dropped items.

DRAIN CLEANING

What's the best way to keep your drains flowing? Pour some boiling water down a drain about once a week. Heat about a gallon, pour in half, wait a few minutes, then pour in the rest. Be careful to pour the water directly down into the drain rather than in the basin, because boiling water may crack porcelain fixtures.

If a drain becomes clogged despite the boiling-water treatment, there are chemical drain cleaners you can use. But these cleaners are among the most hazardous consumer products available. Most of them are strongly corrosive alkalies or concentrated acids, and open a blocked drain by eating and boiling their way through the clog. Such strong chemicals can severely damage your eyes, lungs, and skin. Accidentally swallowing even a small amount of drain opener can result in injury or even death. It is far safer and no less effective to use a mechanical device to clear a clogged drain.

Try a rubber plunger first. It's cheap, easy to use, and usually works. A second alternative is a product that uses pressurized air or gas to push an obstruction around the bend in the drainpipe and into the clear. But beware of the pressure if you have old, corroded drain lines.

Stubborn clogs call for the services of a licensed plumber to avoid damaging yourself or the plumbing.

Dryers *(see Clothes Dryers)*

ELECTRIC SHOCK

A plugged-in, hand-held hair dryer and other portable appliances that are accidentally dropped into a bathtub or washbasin will electrify the water and create a lethal shock hazard. This is usually true even if the appliance is switched off.

Under an Underwriters Laboratories (UL) standard, hair dryers, at least, must have a significant degree of built-in safety against such an electrical hazard.

In one design, the switch is encapsulated in material that keeps water away from any electrically live parts if the appliance is switched off. The protection isn't total, however. A child who pulls an appliance into bath water and manages to turn it on still risks electrocution. The antishock standard is, nevertheless, a major improvement.

For safety's sake, bathroom electrical outlets should be replaced with the kind that have a ground-fault circuit interrupter. This device cuts off power if it senses even a tiny current leak, thus providing the best protection. Without a ground-fault device, using any electrical device in a bathroom is a classic example of an accident waiting to happen—unless the device is specifically made for such use and is protected by appropriate design safeguards. If this is the case, the product will be so labeled.

ELECTRONIC TYPEWRITERS

Manual typewriters and old-fashioned electrics—the kind that's basically a manual typewriter with a power assist—have given way to the electronic typewriter.

The electronic typewriter streamlines routine typing chores such as starting a new line, making corrections, and setting margins and tabs. It can check your spelling, file a few pages in its memory and print what it has stored on command, and correct typographical errors at the touch of a key. But the typical electronic typewriter is not a computer word processor. Some electronic machines still just type directly on the paper. Those with a memory store what you type and spew it out line by line after you've completed and corrected the document. But you are limited to viewing a small "window" of text, typically only 20 characters wide. By contrast, a typical computer monitor can show up to 2,000 characters at once.

Some other features and considerations:

• *Impact-printing* models use an element whose fully formed characters strike the ribbon. *Thermal-printing* typewriters use a grid of tiny pins or rods to transfer each character's image to the paper. The thermal printers don't print quite as crisply as the impact printers, and they are unable to make carbon copies.

• The cost of producing a page of typewritten material with an electronic machine is considerable. The typical film ribbon should be good for about 25 pages, assuming that 2,000 characters are typed per page. At $5 a ribbon, that comes to about 20 cents per page.

• Features that push a typewriter's price upward are text memory, a large correction memory, a large display, and a spelling checker. Other useful features include automatic centering, automatic underlining, and index and express-backspace keys.

• In narrowing down your selection, it is very important that you try out the typewriter to see whether the keyboard is comfortable to use. This is not possible to do in all stores, so your shopping may have to be done in two stages: the tryout, and then price shopping for the model that you have finally selected.

EXERCISE AND CALORIES

The number of calories you expend in a given exercise depends on three things: how long you exercise, how vigorously you exercise, and how much you weigh. Exercising harder or faster burns more calories, but the amount of time you spend is just as important as the amount of effort you put into it. Weight also influences the outcome. Other things being equal, a heavier person does more work—and burns more calories—than a lighter person, because more poundage is being hauled around.

When it comes to losing weight, however, the formula is

Activity	Calories expended per hour
Walking at 2 mph	240
Walking at 3 mph	320
Walking at 4.5 mph	440
Bicycling at 6 mph	240
Jogging at 5.5 mph	740
Jogging at 7 mph	920
Running at 10 mph	1,280
Swimming at 25 yd per min	275
Swimming at 50 yd per min	500
Jumping rope	750
Running in place	650
Cross-country skiing	700
Tennis, singles	400

not at all simple. Calorie expenditure is not directly related to how much weight a person loses. Other factors are involved, some of them understood, some not so well understood. Nevertheless, it is helpful to know how many calories you are burning off in a variety of activities.

The table on page 78, issued by the National Institutes of Health, provides this information for a 150-pound person, male or female. For a given activity, a 100-pound person burns approximately one-third fewer calories than a 150-pound person; a 200-pound person burns about one-third more. To adjust the table to your own weight, add or subtract a proportionate amount of calories. If you weigh 125 pounds, for example, subtract 17 percent (half of one-third) from the value shown.

EXERCISE BICYCLES

Bicycling is one of the best aerobic exercises. It strengthens the legs, makes leg and hip muscles more flexible, burns a lot of calories per minute, and conditions the body to use oxygen more efficiently, increasing overall endurance and heart and lung capacity. Riding an exercise bike is also easy if you aren't as well coordinated as you would like to be and need to get back into shape gradually.

Choosing a bike is not so easy. A multitude of brands and models are available. You will probably have to spend at least $150 or $200 for a bike that's sturdy and operates smoothly enough for comfortable riding.

How They Work. All exercise bikes work on the same principle. Pedaling moves the exercise bike's single wheel (which acts as a flywheel to even out the force needed to keep the mechanism moving) against some form of resistance—sort of like riding a bike with the brakes on. You can adjust the resistance, making the bike easier or harder to pedal. On cheap bikes, the wheel looks like a wheel on a regular bicycle. Such wheels develop little momentum and don't do much to make the ride smooth.

Your pulse rate tells you how hard you're working. It's easy to measure while you're riding—just count your pulse for 10 seconds and multiply by 6. To improve cardiovascular conditioning, you need to elevate your pulse rate to 70 to 80 percent of its theoretical maximum (that's the difference between 220 and your age) and keep it there for at least 20 minutes, three times a week. After a while, you'll probably be able to tell when you're working hard enough just by the way you feel.

What to Look For. A smooth, quiet ride is an important attribute of an exercise bike. It needs a rigid frame that doesn't flex and wobble as you pedal.

The next most important influence on the ride is the flywheel. On the best bikes, the flywheel glides with even, steady force as you pump the pedals.

There are two main ways to change the pedaling force. On some bikes, a belt or strap cinched around the flywheel increases the resistance. On other bikes, calipers with pads (like bicycle brakes) pinch the flywheel.

A number of features add to the comfort and convenience of an exercise bike:

• *Seat.* Generally, a wide seat is the most comfortable. A seat that's too narrow makes you rest uncomfortably on your pelvic bone. Many bikes have a seat mounting like the one on regular bikes, which allows you to replace the seat if you want.

• *Resistance control.* This control is generally a knob or a lever. It should be mounted on the handlebars, within easy reach while you are pedaling, and it should be easy to operate. Some controls have no markings. Others merely indicate which direction to turn to increase or decrease resistance. Best are calibrated controls, which allow you to return to the same resistance setting time after time.

• *Odometer and speedometer.* These tell you how "far" you have pedaled and how fast you are pedaling. A timer is a good thing to have as well, since people tend to ride for a certain amount of time rather than for a certain distance.

• *Toe straps.* Pedals with toe straps prevent your feet from slipping off the pedals and enable you to work on both the upstroke and the downstroke. Weighted pedals allow the toe straps to stay on top, making it easy to slip your foot into them.

Try an exercise bike on for size before you buy. The seat should be set so that when the pedal dips to its lowest position, your leg is almost fully extended. This lets you exercise the large leg muscles most efficiently and comfortably—and safely. Habitual use of a bike whose seat is at the wrong height can cause knee injuries.

A final note: If you are over 35 and you have any of the risk factors for heart disease, check with your doctor before you start an exercise program.

EXERCISE GUIDELINES

Runners, joggers, and other exercisers should know that general fatigue, pain, nausea, light-headedness, and dizziness are all signs to slow down. Progressively overloading your aerobic capacity doesn't mean "working through" chest pains until you feel sick. As a maxim, "No pain, no gain" is dangerous advice. Heed these other medical guidelines:

• Any sharp pain or one that occurs during a pounding exercise such as jogging or during the flexing or extension of a joint is a sign to tend to the injury immediately. For strains and pulls, the recommended treatment is "RICE" (rest, ice, compression, elevation).

• People in good health are probably safe in starting an exercise program on their own. Those over 35 or those who have had health problems should get a doctor's go-ahead first.

• People with high blood pressure should seek their doctor's advice before taking up rowing or weight training. Working the chest and arm muscles against resistance temporarily raises the blood pressure, perhaps dangerously so in people who already have a problem. Breathing correctly can help: exhale during the exertion, inhale during the recovery.

• Anyone with a bad knee or a bad back should proceed cautiously. Those people should seek advice from their orthopedist, physiatrist, or exercise physiologist. The straight-leg sit-ups recommended in many rowing machine instructions should be avoided by all except those with very strong abdominal muscles, as should most sit-up techniques recommended for home gyms.

FABRIC PILL REMOVERS

Pilling, that annoying and unsightly accumulation of fuzz balls, commonly occurs when fibers are worked loose from a fabric by rubbing. The resulting "pills" are held in place by fibers that still hold firm. Loosely woven and knitted synthetics and blends are especially apt to pill, but woolens aren't immune. Pills can form on clothes, blankets, and upholstery fabrics, but sweaters seem especially vulnerable.

Some new gadgets on the market that remove pills include a miniature electric shaver run by a dry-cell battery that drives a fan-shaped cutting blade. The blade sweeps behind a screen with holes large enough for most pills to poke through. The shaver, in effect, beheads the pill. Shavers work best on small pills, especially those on fabrics that don't have a nap.

Another device is a snagger with a rough surface that snags the pills and rips them off. A snagger works best on large pills—those on firmly constructed materials such as overcoating and heavy weaves. It can also restore the nap on fabrics.

If you have sweaters with light pilling and an overcoat with heavy pilling, you will need both a shaver and a snagger. However, the shavers work better than snaggers on stretchy knits, which tend to be pulled and distorted by a snagger.

One dry cleaner says that the fastest and most reliable way

to remove pills is to use a common safety razor, shaving the pilled area as one would shave skin. If you decide to try this method, *be very careful.*

FABRIC SOFTENERS

You wouldn't need a fabric softener at all if it weren't for synthetic detergents, which tend to leave clothes feeling scratchy. Regular soap has a softening effect, largely because it doesn't rinse out of textiles as thoroughly as detergents do. Fabric softeners work by coating fabric fibers, much as hair conditioners coat hair, leaving a thin layer of waxy or soapy substance that makes the fabric feel "soft." The coating also separates a napped fabric's fibers and stands them on end, making the laundry fluff up. After testing more than a dozen softeners of every type, we've come up with the following hints:

• Fabric softeners tend to work better in hard water than in soft. It's best to use fabric softener in the rinse cycle, after the detergent has done its work, or in the dryer.

• Detergent/softener combinations present a problem: the chemicals used for softening tend to neutralize the chemicals used for cleaning. Manufacturers have tried to solve this problem in various ways, but the compromises seem to work only at some cost to both cleaning and softening.

• Static cling is caused by the tumbling action of a clothes dryer, which causes electrical charges to build up on the surface of synthetic fabrics. A thin coating of fabric softener disrupts the buildup.

• You'll get best results, particularly if wash is done in hard water, with softener-impregnated dryer sheets. But the sheets must be used with caution. They generally carry a warning to use low-heat settings for synthetics and blends (oily spots may appear at higher heat, or if there are only a few items in the load). Liquids can also cause spotting if they are poured directly onto clothes. The remedy for softener spots is to moisten the fabric, rub the spot with a bar of plain soap, and wash again.

FAST FOOD

Many people seem to throw their nutritional caution to the winds when eating out. Perhaps that's because people view eating out more as an entertainment, reserving good nutrition for eating at home.

This approach can work if you and your family rarely eat fast food. A steady diet of typical fast-food items will overload you with protein, fat, and calories while shortchanging you on minerals and fiber. To balance one meal of burger, shake, and fries, you'd have to search out low-fat, vitamin- and mineral-rich fare the rest of the day.

But by choosing from a fast-food menu wisely, you can put together a fairly well balanced meal. Here are some tips on how to do that:

• Choose roast beef over hamburgers if you can. Roast beef is often leaner than a burger and can be quite tasty. By adding tomato, lettuce, and such, you can enhance the meal with extra nutrients.

• Choose small, plain hamburgers instead of the giant, mouth-filling variety with all the works. Skip the mayonnaise and cheese. Passing up the mayonnaise can save around 150 calories. Cheese, while a source of protein and calcium, also contains fat.

• Choose regular fried chicken, not the "extra crispy" recipe. Extra fat adds the crispness—probably as much as 100 calories per piece.

• Order milk instead of a shake. Low-fat milk provides

much more protein and calcium per calorie than a fast-food shake. Or order a diet soda.

• If your object is to cut calories, go easy on the french-fried potatoes. Split an order with someone else. Or, if it's available, order a plain baked potato instead.

• Choose a fast-food salad. If you try a boxed salad, one with chicken or shrimp will supply some protein along with the fiber, complex carbohydrates, vitamins, and minerals from the vegetables. At a salad bar choose carrots, tomatoes, and dark green vegetables. And go easy on dressings, fatty croutons, taco chips, and mayonnaise-laden pasta and potato salads.

FIBER IN THE DIET

Dietary fiber, sometimes called roughage, is the indigestible part of plant foods—fruits, vegetables, grains, and legumes. It adds bulk to the feces and may help to prevent constipation, hemorrhoids, and diverticulitis (a common, and occasionally serious, intestinal disorder). But these good effects aren't what's creating all the furor over fiber. Rather, it's fiber's reported potential for reducing the risk of cancer of the colon.

Among all cancers, colon cancer is second only to lung cancer in its toll on American lives. Every year, physicians diagnose some 90,000 cases, and only about half of those survive five or more years after diagnosis. Thus, there's good reason to pay attention to dietary measures that might reduce the risk of the disease.

Recent Studies. The Department of Health and Human Services has said that if Americans ate less fat and more fiber, cases of colon cancer in the United States could fall by 30 percent, saving some 20,000 lives each year.

The Canadian government, the U.S. Department of Agri-

This table shows estimated fiber content (in grams) for a number of high-fiber foods. Estimates from various sources often vary, not only because of the inherent variability within food samples but also because there is as yet no standardized test method for simulating the human digestive process. The list shown here is excerpted from the Nutrition Action Healthletter, *April 1986, published by the Center for Science in the Public Interest.*

Legumes (½ cup)	Dietary fiber
Kidney beans	5.8 gm
Pinto beans	5.3
Split peas	5.1
White beans	5.0
Lima beans	4.9

Vegetables (usually ½ cup)	
Sweet potato (1 large)	4.2 gm
Peas	4.1
Brussels sprouts	3.9
Corn	3.9
Potato, baked (1 medium)	3.8
Carrots (1 raw or ½ cup cooked)	2.3
Collards	2.2
Asparagus	2.1
Green beans	2.1
Broccoli	2.0
Spinach	2.0
Turnips	1.7
Mushrooms, raw	0.9
Summer squash	0.7
Lettuce, raw	0.3

Grains (usually 1 oz)	Dietary fiber
Brown rice, cooked (½ cup)	2.4 gm
Millet, cooked (½ cup)	1.8
Whole-wheat bread (1 slice)	1.6
Rye bread (1 slice)	1.0
Spaghetti, cooked (½ cup)	0.8
White bread (1 slice)	0.6
White rice, cooked (½ cup)	0.1

Fruits	
Blackberries (½ cup)	4.5 gm
Prunes, dried (3)	3.7
Apple with skin (1)	2.6
Banana (1 medium)	2.0
Strawberries (¾ cup)	2.0
Grapefruit (½ medium)	1.7
Peach (1 medium)	1.6
Cantaloupe (¼ small)	1.4
Raisins (2 tbsp)	1.3
Orange (1 small)	1.2
Grapes	0.5

Sources: Anderson, J. "Plant Fiber in Foods." (HCF Diabetes Research Foundation, Inc. P.O. Box 22124, Lexington, KY 40522) 1986.
USDA Handbook #8-8.
USDA Nutrient Data Research Group, personal communication.
Product-label information.

culture (USDA), and the National Cancer Institute, among others, have also suggested that people eat more fiber.

Most of the evidence for fiber's anticancer effect comes from epidemiological studies—that is, studies of diseases as they appear in populations of people. The first hint that fiber could protect against cancer came to public attention in 1974, when Denis P. Burkitt, a British physician, and his colleagues reported that rural Africans, who suffer much less colon cancer than Americans, typically consume much more fiber (50 to 150 grams per day) than Americans (10 to 20 grams per day) do.

In another study, researchers found that Danes in Copenhagen, who consumed an average of 17 grams of fiber per day, suffered from three times as much colon cancer as the Finns of Kuopio, who consumed an average of 31 grams per day. Similar correlations have been shown in Great Britain, Connecticut, and elsewhere, although not consistently. In general, the key difference between the populations under study appeared to be in their consumption of insoluble fiber found in whole-grain cereals and whole-grain baked goods.

Also, people on vegetarian or semivegetarian diets—which often contain high levels of a variety of fiber types—have a low incidence of colon cancer.

FILM PROCESSING

An expert photographer may use a professional processing laboratory that gives special (and costly) attention to each one of his or her prints. But more ordinary snapshooters have three main processing choices. You can use a mail-order processor and wait a week or so. Or you can drop off film at a supermarket, drugstore, camera store, or kiosk for pickup in one or two days. Either way, the film is generally processed at a big laboratory that handles thousands of rolls a day. A third alternative is the so-called minilab—a retail outlet that does the processing on the premises and commonly offers finished prints in as little as an hour. While they are fast, minilabs tend to be expensive compared with mail-order processing.

The main drawback to mail-order film processing is the time it takes to get your prints back. And solving problems that require reprinting can be awkward from a distance. There's also a small risk in sending film through the mail.

No matter where you have film processed, machines do most, if not all, of the labor. Finished prints are sliced off the paper roll as they come out of the printer. While someone at the lab ought to inspect the prints for processing defects, many labs may skip that step, or do it only cursorily, depending on the work load. Therefore, it's important to examine your pictures carefully when you get them back. The following tips may help you to get the prints you want:

• If a print is unsatisfactory, check the negative. You can't expect a processor to be able to do much with a badly exposed negative. But if the image on the negative has good contrast, ask to have the print remade. Give the lab clear, written instructions: "the flower should be lavender, not dark purple" or "background is dark red; print so face in foreground has normal flesh tones." Ordinarily, you won't have to pay for remakes to replace a bad print.

• Try to keep film cool, particularly between the time it was exposed and the time it is developed. Latent images on exposed film can deteriorate over time, particularly in hot, humid weather. Don't let a roll sit in the camera for a month while you're waiting to take the last shot or two, and don't leave your camera or film in the sun or in an enclosed hot car.

• On a vacation in a hot climate, consider having your pictures developed promptly, rather than waiting until you return home. Take a mailer along and send the film to the lab of your choice.

• Handle negatives as little as possible. Never touch the part with the image. When selecting negatives for reprinting or enlargement, send the whole strip; never cut the negatives apart. Fill out the return envelope before the negatives are inserted in order to prevent pressure from the pen from damaging the negative.

• There's no remedy for film that's ruined by the processor. The best you can expect is a new roll, with free processing.

• If your film is lost, it may turn up again, particularly if you've put your name and address on the cartridge.

FINANCIAL PLANNING

Financial planners have long served wealthy individuals. Now planners are offering middle-income folks strategies for cutting taxes, choosing investments, and the like. Planners may be independent and work out of an office at home or they may be affiliated with large, well-known companies and work out of a skyscraper on Wall Street. Some are lawyers or accountants who write financial plans as a sideline, hoping you'll send your tax or legal business their way.

You can also buy financial plans from insurance companies or brokerage firms. In some cases, you sit down with a planner and chat face-to-face about your financial needs. In others, you fill out a questionnaire and get your plan back in the mail.

Planning itself may be a service, but it inevitably leads to the purchase of financial products—stocks, bonds, certificates of deposit, insurance policies, etc. Many planners, therefore, often turn out to have hidden agendas—selling mutual funds, for example, or life insurance, or tax-preparation services.

The following are some of the hallmarks of a well-drawn financial plan:

- It is written in understandable language.
- The recommendations are clear and unambiguous.
- It contains a cash-flow analysis, a kind of budget that shows your income from all sources, minus all your expenses.
- There is a net-worth statement (a summary of your assets and liabilities).
- It examines your current debts to see if they should be consolidated, paid off from other available funds, or refinanced.
- It includes an examination of your current insurance and recommends ways to bolster your coverage (if necessary) and to save on premiums (if possible).
- It examines your current investment portfolio and makes recommendations for restructuring your investments, if appropriate.
- It includes a tax analysis and tax-saving suggestions.
- It touches on retirement planning and estate planning.
- It includes a statement of your goals, objectives, and tolerance for investment risk.

Planners shouldn't plan and run. They should offer assistance in putting recommendations into effect or coordinating the implementation with others, such as a lawyer who might draw up a will for you. They should periodically review the plan with you to see if changing circumstances have made it, or parts of it, obsolete.

Fingernails (*see Brittle Nails*)

FIRE EXTINGUISHERS
Can you tell, in advance, how well a fire extinguisher will work? Yes, indeed. Most extinguishers on the market today carry an Underwriters Laboratories (UL) rating. A reliable

guide to performance, the rating is in the form of a set of numbers and letters that tell you what type and size of fire the unit can handle.

An extinguisher with a 1A rating must, among other things, be able to put out a blazing test stack of 50 pieces of 20-inch-long wood two-by-twos. A 2A model must be able to put out a fire twice that size. A 1B rating means a model can extinguish 3¼ gallons of liquid fuel burning in a 2½-square-foot pan. A C rating (this letter is never preceded by a number) means the unit's chemical contents are nonconductive and therefore safe to use on electrical fires.

Extinguishers that use finely powdered ammonium phosphate are called "all-purpose" or "multipurpose" models. They are effective against wood, fuel, and electrical fires, but despite their versatility they aren't necessarily the best choice.

An extinguisher that uses sodium bicarbonate is better in the kitchen, where grease fires are common. The chemical smothers burning grease much faster and more thoroughly than does ammonium phosphate.

Ammonium phosphate and sodium bicarbonate both leave behind a messy, corrosive residue, the sort of material you don't want left on hi-fi equipment or on a computer. A halon fire extinguisher, which uses halon gases to choke off a fire, leaves no messy residue. Halon also doesn't conduct electricity and is therefore suitable for a class C electrical fire, as well as class B fires. Larger halon models work on class A fires, too.

Think of halon models as auxiliary fire extinguishers. Since they leave no residue, they are unequaled in protecting prized objects. But they are expensive, and most are probably too small to be the only protection in a garage or workshop.

Dry-chemical models are not only cheaper to buy, they are also cheaper to recharge. Regardless of the extinguishing chemical used, recharging costs almost as much as a new fire extinguisher, especially if the model is a small one. It makes sense to replace a small unit if its pressure drops too much or if it's been used.

Conveniences. A fire extinguisher should be virtually foolproof to maintain and convenient to operate. Look for the following features:

Mounting. Heavier models hang from a wall-mounted hook. Lighter units are strapped to a plate that's screwed to the wall. A few are designed to be held in place with a Velcro self-adhesive strip, but the adhesive isn't likely to hold well except on a very smooth surface. A mounting bracket should be designed to hold the extinguisher in place securely; just as important, it should release the extinguisher quickly and easily.

Pressure Indicator. Because a fire extinguisher may not be used for years, you should check it monthly to be sure it remains properly pressurized. The best pressure indicator is a dial-and-pointer-type gauge; a glance at the dial tells you if the unit is pressurized as it should be. Some units have a plastic push-pin indicator. If the pin pops up after you push it, pressure is adequate.

Dual-halon models are unlikely to have a pressure indicator. You check pressure by weighing the unit. This is a drawback, because the weight must be precise to a fraction of an ounce; household scales usually aren't capable of such precision.

Tamper Seal. Any fire extinguisher should have some kind of device to prevent accidental firing. But any such seal should be easy to remove, a necessity for saving precious fire-fighting time.

Firing Mechanism. To fire most of the larger dry-chemical models, you have to squeeze a pair of levers. This can require substantial effort. These models won't suit you unless you have a very firm grip.

Instructions. An extinguisher should be marked with easy-to-read words and pictures that show at a glance the steps to follow.

Every home should have a sodium-bicarbonate extinguisher in the kitchen, where most home fires begin. Buy an all-purpose extinguisher for protecting the garage, the workshop, and other areas. It's a good idea to keep one under the driver's seat of a car.

Safety. If there's a fire, get the family to safety and call the fire department. If you can't get closer than 10 or 12 feet, the fire is probably too big to tackle and you should leave immediately. The burning materials and the chemical reactions under way during burning may generate toxic byproducts; gases from the extinguishing agent may also be noxious.

Finally, even if the fire seems small enough to fight, stay close to a door or window that allows for a speedy exit. Remember, too, that the first burst from the fire extinguisher may not do the job. If the fire hasn't been smothered completely, the flames may erupt again.

FISH AND HEALTH (*see also* OILS AND FATS FOR COOKING)

Studies show that Eskimos' platelets (blood cells involved in clotting) are less sticky than those of Europeans or Americans, and don't clump together as readily. Eskimos' well-known resistance to coronary disease may be linked to this difference—the less sticky platelets are less likely to form a clot, or "thrombus," that could cause a heart attack by blocking a coronary artery. The factor that protects Eskimos from coronary disease may be their high intake of certain fatty acids in their diet, notably those found in fish.

All fats, solid or liquid, are composed of various combinations of fatty acids. The types and amounts of acids present are what makes one fat different from another. One molecular group of polyunsaturated fatty acids—called the omega-

6 group—is abundant in land plants. Another—the omega-3 group—is more plentiful in sea plants, especially in cold waters.

Fish Oil. Fish are a good source of omega-3 fatty acids because fish eat sea plants—or eat other fish that do. Generally, the colder the water and the oilier the fish, the greater the omega-3 content.

Like other fatty acids, the omega-3 variety enters the membranes of many body cells, including the platelets. One omega-3 type acid common in fish oil is eicosapentaenoic acid, or, simply, EPA. Research has indicated that sufficient intake of EPA can compete with arachidonic acid, an omega-6 fatty acid involved in the formation of substances that make platelets sticky.

The effect on platelets is not confined to the Eskimo diet. Japanese fishermen consuming large amounts of fish daily also exhibit reduced platelet stickiness. Like the Eskimos, the fishing group experiences a very low rate of coronary disease.

The succession of favorable reports about the beneficial effects of seafood in the diet reached a crescendo in 1985 when the *New England Journal of Medicine* published three studies supporting the possible benefits of seafood. Prominently featured was a report from the Netherlands that fish consumption may lower the risk of fatal heart attack. Some 850 men in the town of Zutphen had been followed for 20 years to assess various risk factors in heart disease. A major finding was that fish consumption was associated with a reduced rate of fatal coronaries. Men who ate roughly 7 to 11 ounces of fish weekly had less than half the coronary death rate of men who ate no fish at all. Men who consumed more than 11 ounces of fish a week—about a pound, on average—experienced virtually the same reduction in risk as those who ate 7 to 11 ounces. There was no extra advantage to the higher level of intake.

Some 16 percent of Americans never eat fish, and another 19 percent eat it less than once a month. Even if it hasn't been proved conclusively that fish is good for the heart, there's still ample room in a well-balanced diet for its inclusion.

Caution. Some people are allergic to fish, and become ill from eating even a small amount. For most people, however, there isn't much to worry about in having a few fish meals a week, providing the fish don't come from polluted waters containing chemicals or other contaminants. When eating raw shellfish, for example, there is a risk of hepatitis or food poisoning. If you're in an area where outbreaks have been traced to shellfish, avoid eating any raw mollusks or other shellfish. Always steam clams for at least 4 to 6 minutes, not just until the shells open.

Eating raw fish, such as sushi or sashimi, also involves a risk, mainly from an intestinal parasite known as the fish tapeworm. Although ocean fish usually present no problem, lake fish and Alaskan salmon are sometimes infected. Accordingly, if you prepare raw fish yourself, stick to ocean varieties. In restaurants, inquire about the source of the fish before ordering.

Federal regulations that limit contaminant residues in fish don't apply to sport fish such as lake trout. Try to avoid those taken from lakes or streams known to have pollution problems.

Fetuses are most vulnerable to mercury toxicity. It's possible for a pregnant woman to exceed the permissible level of mercury intake if she eats a lot of fish, particularly large predators such as swordfish, tuna, red snapper, freshwater trout, and northern pike.

FLASHLIGHTS: RECHARGEABLE

A standard flashlight won't be of much use in an emergency unless its disposable batteries are working well. In this respect, a rechargeable light has much to recommend it: in the event of a power outage, the light will be close at hand with its batteries fully charged.

Most convenient are models that can remain plugged into their charging stand or wall outlet, taking a "trickle charge" when not in use. Models that can't be trickle-charged may be less than fully charged when they're needed.

A rechargeable flashlight should be compact, convenient to carry, and easy to store. Rechargeable lanterns are bulkier and heavier than flashlights, but are usually more powerful.

The brightest lights use a krypton or a halogen bulb. These bulbs cost 4 or 5 times more to replace than ordinary incandescent bulbs, but they are well worth the money if brightness is your main concern. (Sometimes the length of time a light remains lit is more important than the brightness. Some lights offer a low-power setting that gives you a dimmer light for a longer period of time.)

Variable Light Pattern. You may want to illuminate a large area all at once. Some models can switch from a narrow, concentrated beam to a wider (though dimmer) beam.

Angle Adjustment. Some lanterns, or their reflectors, can be pivoted up or down, which is handy when the lantern is resting on a flat surface.

Magnet. Some flashlights have a magnet that holds them to a metal surface such as a car body.

Charge-Indicator Light. This important feature tells whether the light is actually charging.

Cylindrical Shape. While it makes sense for a flashlight to be cylindrical, this design can turn into a deficiency when you try to set the flashlight down on an inclined surface only to see it rolling away. There should be some flat surfaces on the cylinder to prevent this from happening.

Batteries. Nickel-cadmium batteries should be good for about 1,000 recharges. Proper care requires that the cells be

almost completely discharged from time to time. Otherwise, they "remember" only the partial charge and eventually
refuse a fuller charge. For example, if you repeatedly recharge nickel-cadmium batteries after only a half hour of use,
you'll eventually *have* to recharge them after every half hour
of use.

Lights with lead-acid batteries require different treatment.
One maker says that if you use the light until it dims, the
batteries may be good for only 200 recharges; but, with regular recharging after only 40 minutes' use, the light may last
for 2,000 recharges.

FOOD PROCESSORS

A food processor can be the workhorse of the kitchen—it can
chop, slice, grind, blend, puree, shred, mix, and knead. But
a full-size processor isn't for everyone. Overall, a compact
model can do as well as a big machine if you routinely deal
with smaller amounts of food. The bowl of a compact model
holds 2 cups less than that of a full-size one. For light use, a
good compact unit should serve quite well. It handles many
chores competently, and it's smaller, lighter, and easier to
store than a large machine.

Food processor owners often say their machine is the preferred appliance for only a few tasks: making coleslaw, mayonnaise, or bread and cracker crumbs; pureeing vegetables
for soup; and grating hard cheese. They are less likely to use
a processor for such common chores as chopping onions or
celery and slicing or chopping other vegetables. One possible
reason for the limited use is that owners often feel it's just
not worth the trouble to take out the machine from storage
and assemble it for smaller jobs. And they shy away from
having to clean the processor after small slicing and chopping
jobs.

A food processor can be a boon, but you will be able to take
advantage of a machine's versatility only if you can find a

permanent place for it on a countertop, so that it is available for use at a moment's notice.

Convenience. Some food processors are easier to live with than others. The most convenient ones are easy to assemble, disassemble, and clean. Here are some additional details on the desirable features of most food processors:

Bowl. All bowls are of clear plastic, usually with a handle. The bowl has in its base an open-topped tube that accommodates the drive shaft for the cutting blade. The tube's height can limit how much liquid the bowl can hold. The chopping or mixing blade fits over the tube, but it usually doesn't form a tight seal, so there's a chance of leakage around the bowl's lid during processing. A bowl can hold more dry ingredients.

In time, a bowl's transparency may dim and the plastic can become cloudy, particularly if the machine is used for processing a lot of dry or semidry foods, which have a mildly abrasive effect on the plastic, causing minute scratches.

Continuous Feed. A food chute on most compacts and on some large models lets you feed in food continuously, sending the sliced or shredded results out the chute into a plate or bowl alongside. This arrangement lets you process a lot of food but also gives you an extra package of accessories to store.

Feed Tube. Most models have an open tube in the bowl's lid, through which food can be fed. A large feed tube will hold a lot of vegetables, for example, for slicing or shredding. And it can support small bits, such as a single carrot or pepperoni stick, so the food won't fall over. However, feed-tube assemblies are cumbersome to put together and difficult to clean.

Food Pusher. The pusher guides the food down the feed tube and into contact with the blade. Those food pushers with graduated markings can double as measuring cups; the handiest ones are transparent.

Blades, Disks. Standard equipment includes an S-shaped metal chopping blade, a slicing disk, and a shredding disk. In some models, the slicers and shredders are separate; in others, they're combined on a single, reversible disk.

Speeds. While some full-size models offer a selection of speeds, most have only one. A single speed, operated continuously or pulsed on and off, is enough to perform most chores.

Controls. Even with their switch turned on, most full-size models have a safety interlock that prevents them from running until the lid is securely latched.

Cleaning. Machines with clean lines, smooth surfaces, and an absence of food-trapping gaps around switches and trim are the easiest to clean. Many manufacturers suggest cleaning the components in a dishwasher.

Storage. A food processor can be a major competitor for limited countertop space. A full-size unit is a little bigger than an automatic drip coffee maker and usually stands about 13 to 15 inches tall when set up for operation. Compact models are better in this respect, usually taking up about as much space as a blender.

In the cupboard, the machines' extra disks and such also need storage room. And compacts need extra space for their separate chute assembly. You can generally reduce a machine's storage height by inverting the lid to point the feed tube into the bowl.

Safety. Be careful with disks and blades that must be stored apart from the machine—their sharp edges can inflict a nasty gash. It's not a good idea to put them into a drawer with other kitchen tools, where people reaching in might cut themselves.

Some machines have disks with finger grips or holes, to help minimize your contact with the blades, and some models' chopping blades have tall hubs with a knob for a safer grip. Other models force you to deal directly with sharp edges: they have slicing and shredding inserts that must be slid or snapped into a plastic disk before you can use them.

The blades of most machines stop spinning in 2½ seconds or less after you remove the lid.

FOOD PROCESSORS: MINI

Minis are cylindrical little gadgets intended for small, light kitchen jobs—chopping herbs, onions, or a clove or two of garlic. They can't process much at a time, and they can't slice, shred, or handle some other chores that are easy for a larger machine.

Some people who live alone might find a mini-processor of some use. But a knife or a grater can probably do just as well.

FOOD STORAGE

Some people leave hot foods uncovered to cool before storing them in the refrigerator. Prompt refrigeration, however, is a good safety precaution. The danger is that if any bacteria survive the cooking process, they'll proliferate much faster if the food is allowed to cool at room temperature for an hour or two before being refrigerated.

But food poisoning is not often a problem in home cooking; it's more common in commercial or institutional facilities, where food is handled in bulk quantities. So allowing small portions of food to cool for a while, the old-fashioned way, is unlikely to pose a threat—unless it sits there too long.

Whether you refrigerate the food or not (we suggest you do), though, be sure to cover it. Leaving food uncovered can hasten spoilage by exposing it to microorganisms in the air. In fact, cover any food you intend to store, whether you let it cool awhile or not. A pot cover or paper towel can help protect it. Covering food can also prevent it from picking up other cooking odors—a hint of garlic won't enhance your custard pie or chocolate pudding.

If you want to seal hot food in plastic wrap or foil, wait until it has cooled; this will help prevent excessive moisture condensation.

Frankfurters *(see Hot Dogs)*

Fraud *(see Mail-order Fraud; Telephone Fraud)*

FREEZERS

A well-stocked freezer can be a great convenience, especially for a large family. But it can also cause you to waste money. Without proper wrapping, frozen food can suffer "freezer burn" or dehydration. And without proper rotation of your stock, you can ruin a lot of food. Frozen food is ultimately perishable, and too long a stay in the freezer can make the tastiest of foods inedible.

Managing Your Freezer. It takes only a little extra time and organization to manage a freezer wisely:

• *Use a freezer thermometer*. When you install the freezer, leave the thermometer in the center of the empty compartment for at least a day to make sure the freezer is working properly. Depending on the reading, adjust the temperature control and aim for a reading of 0°F. Recheck the temperature in winter and summer, and reset the thermostat higher or lower if necessary.

• *Learn which foods freeze best*. Check the freezer's manual, or send for the U.S. Department of Agriculture's booklet *Home Freezing of Fruits and Vegetables*. (It's item 142M. The address is: Consumer Information Center (P), PO Box 100, Pueblo, CO 81002.) Nutritionally, meat, fish, poultry, and eggs are the same frozen or fresh, while fruits and vegetables lose vitamins if they're not handled properly before freezing.

• *Wrap food securely*. Plastic wrap should be vapor-proof.

You can also use aluminum foil or plastic containers with snap-on lids. Don't rely on waxed paper, butcher's paper, regular polyethylene plastic wrap, or even cardboard ice cream cartons. Rewrap all supermarket-packaged meat. Try to expel as much air as possible from a package before you seal it. Freezer tape, rubber bands, twist ties, or even string can seal the wrapping.

• *Label packages with their contents, serving size, and the date of freezing.* The date is especially important so you can use up a food before it's been in the freezer too long. Try to balance the flow of food into the freezer with the flow out; this is one way to ensure that no foods stay frozen too long. Move the oldest packages to the top or front.

• *Thaw food in the refrigerator.* If you must speed the thawing process, run lukewarm water over the package or use the Defrost setting on your microwave oven. Never refreeze thawed-out food.

• *Defrost the freezer when the frozen-food supply is low.* Transfer the remaining food to your refrigerator's freezer or to the refrigerator itself. Or wrap the food in layers of newspaper while you defrost. Use pans of hot water and a small fan to speed up the process. Never use a knife, ice pick, or other sharp object to loosen ice and frost; you could seriously damage the cooling system.

FROZEN ENTRÉES

Many people eat frozen entrées now and then, especially in those homes where both partners work. These consumers don't expect much in the way of a gourmet experience; they prefer convenience to taste.

The frozen entrée you pick from the supermarket freezer case is certainly unlikely to taste homemade. But if all you want is a hot dish that's fairly cheap and easily prepared, you can find frozen entrées on the market that combine respectable taste, reasonable price, and fairly good nutrition. Besides, you can always supplement a frozen entrée meal with a salad, or with some whole-grain bread. Both will add carbohydrates (and fiber) to the meal and tip the balance of nutrients more favorably.

You may well have to add extra food just to get enough to eat. A big complaint about frozen entrées, besides their bland taste, is their small portions. Most frozen entrées will leave you hungry, since most provide less than 400 calories a serving, even if you don't count on each meal to provide you with one-third or so of the day's calories.

Some entrées also have relatively high sodium levels, which come from additives like the flavor enhancer monosodium glutamate (MSG), as well as from salt. The most sodium-laden entrées give you a dose of more than 1,400 milligrams—the National Research Council says that 1,100 to 3,300 milligrams of sodium is sufficient and safe for most adults for an entire day.

FURNACES

New developments in home heating units can cut your fuel bills substantially. Over a heating season, your present furnace may misdirect as much as half of the heat you've paid for. But modern, high-efficiency designs deliver nearly all the heat content of their fuel to your living spaces. Even a furnace costing $2,000 or more can pay for itself rather quickly.

A new, high-efficiency furnace isn't for everyone. Unless you live in a particularly cold area or have unusually high energy costs, it probably doesn't pay to discard a recently purchased functioning furnace for a high-efficiency model. But if your furnace is more than 15 years old, an investment in a new high-efficiency unit can make sense.

Efficiency. Combustion efficiency (CE), or steady-state efficiency (SEE), is the percentage of a fuel's energy that's converted into usable heat when a furnace operates continuously.

CE is what a technician tests when tuning your furnace. CE measures only operating (or on-time) losses, so it doesn't tell you much about overall fuel use (there are also losses when a furnace cycles off). A better measure is the annual fuel utilization efficiency (AFUE), the percentage of the fuel's energy converted to usable heat over a full year's operation. The AFUE takes into account both on-time and off-time losses; it provides a good basis for comparing furnaces.

High-efficiency furnaces are available with an AFUE of 90 percent and above. If you now own a 15-year-old furnace, its AFUE is probably about 55 percent (if gas-fueled) or about 60 percent (if oil-fueled). You can boost these figures—but only a bit—by modifying the furnace. We tell you how below.

Use the worksheet on page 106 to figure your possible fuel savings in replacing your present gas or oil furnace with a high-efficiency one. There's a sample set of figures (for a home with an annual gas use of 1,600 therms or an oil use of 1,600 gallons) to show how it's done. The worksheet can't be used if you plan to switch fuels.

Upgrading an Existing Furnace. To get more efficiency from an old but still serviceable oil furnace, consider "derating"—that is, using a smaller nozzle, which is likely to boost the AFUE by about 5 percent. Have the derating done as part of your furnace's annual tune-up, which should include a nozzle replacement anyway. If your oil furnace is fairly old, install a flame-retention burner. It may cost as much as $600 to install but can save you 15 to 20 percent a year on fuel.

Derating a gas furnace is not as easy. If you install a smaller nozzle or orifice, you'll also have to modify the flue to restrict the flow of air, which your local building code may not allow.

Replace the pilot light of a gas furnace with an electronic ignition system (which will cost perhaps $200 for hardware and labor). You should save about 5 percent on your annual gas bill.

HEATING WORKSHEET

	Example	Your house
Amount of fuel used now		
1. Number of units of fuel (therms of gas or gallons of oil) used per year.	1,600	_____
2. If some of that fuel is used to produce hot water, put 0.8 here. If none of the fuel is used for hot-water heating, put a 1 here.	× 0.8	_____
3. Multiply line 1 by line 2.	= 1,280	_____
Amount of fuel used by new furnace		
4. Copy the number on line 3 here.	1,280	_____
5. Write the AFUE of your present furnace here. If you don't know what it is, use 55 for gas, 60 for oil.	× 55	_____
6. Multiply line 4 by line 5.	= 70,400	_____
7. Write the AFUE of the new furnace here.	÷ 90	_____
8. Divide line 6 by line 7. The result is the number of units of fuel you'll have to buy to heat your home with the new furnace for a year.	= 782	_____
Annual saving in dollars		
9. Copy the number on line 3 here.	1,280	_____
10. Copy the number on line 8 here.	− 782	_____
11. Subtract line 10 from line 9. The result is the number of units of fuel you can save with the new furnace.	= 498	_____
12. Write the most recent price you paid for a unit of fuel.	× $0.62	_____
13. Multiply line 11 by line 12. The result is the amount you might save per year with the new furnace.	= $309	_____

GARAGE-DOOR OPENERS

People who open a garage door by hand may regard an automatic garage-door opener as a nice extra. But people who own a garage-door opener may well regard it as a necessity of life. Consider: the touch of a button raises the door to admit the car, provides light for unloading passengers or freight, and recloses the door on command. Leaving is equally easy. If you have an attached garage, no more exposing yourself to wind, weather, and dangers in the night.

Today, safety is an important built-in feature in garage-door openers; the most meaningful differences are chiefly extra features and conveniences.

To get the Underwriters Laboratories (UL) seal, a garage-door opener must automatically reverse if the door hits something while descending. (The only exception is if the object is within 1 inch of the ground, so the door can close despite a stray pebble or a buildup of snow.) What if the automatic reverse fails and the door pins someone or something to the ground? To guard against this unlikely event, garage-door openers sold since mid-1982 are supposed to reverse if they can't make the door go all the way down within 30 seconds.

Such safety measures are important. Since 1981, more than a score of children, racing to beat a closing garage door, have been trapped beneath it and killed, according to the Consumer Product Safety Commission. It's important to make sure that the controls, including the transmitters, are kept out of the reach of children. It's also a good idea to operate the door only when you can see it.

GARBAGE BAGS

Garbage bags come in many varieties—trash, rubbish, scrap, kitchen, wastebasket, lawn and leaf. The name, along with some fine print on the package, is supposed to help you pick the right-size bag for your needs. But what about the time you bought "26-gallon" bags that barely fit the 26-gallon can? Some manufacturers measure a bag's capacity when it is filled to the brim; others measure with the bag tied closed. Another reason: without industry-wide standards, some bags won't fit some garbage cans, even though the gallonage is the same for both.

You might think that the thickness of the plastic or the number of plies, as given on the label, would be a good guide to the quality of a bag. That's not so. A bag 2 mils (or 0.002 inch) thick may be weaker than a bag 1.3 mil thick. Paying more and buying the thickest bags you can find are no guarantees you'll get a strong bag.

If a cheaper bag turns out to meet your needs and is strong enough most of the time but not for an occasional heavy load, try double-bagging (slipping one bag inside the other) for those challenging occasions.

GAS BARBECUE GRILLS

The least efficient gas grill is cheaper to run than a kettle-type charcoal grill of similar size. Even if you stint on briquettes, a charcoal grill will still cost more to run than a gas grill.

Of course, a gas grill costs more to buy and may impose some hidden costs as well. The model you select should come with its own fuel tank, which will otherwise cost you an extra

$25 or so. The tank must be purged of air before its first filling, a service that may cost you a couple of dollars. An inaccurate fuel gauge on the tank may also cost you some money, since the charge for filling is the same regardless of how much gas is left in the tank.

Features. When shopping for a gas grill, don't be swayed by such frills as a window in the lid, a temperature gauge, or a timer. More important are handy shelves and racks, an easy-to-change fuel tank, twin burners, an igniter, and split cooking grids. (Two small grids are easier to clean than one large one.)

Assembly. It takes substantial effort and some time to set up a gas grill. Even if you are mechanically adept, you might prefer to have a dealer set up your grill; some dealers will take on the job at no charge. If a grill has damaged or missing parts, a dealer is better able to cope with the situation than you are.

If possible, have the gas-pressure regulator checked and adjusted; it isn't at all unlikely that a brand-new grill will let gas pass at a higher pressure than it should.

Ask the dealer to light the grill as well. Make sure that the igniter will fire the burners in at least 4 seconds. The burners' flames should be blue with a touch of yellow at their tips; if the flames are all blue or all soft yellow, the shutter that regulates the air/fuel ratio needs adjustment.

Cleaning. A thrifty way to clean the grids is by using the gas flame: Before cooking, run the grill on High for about 15 minutes. Then put on oven mitts and other suitable protection and scrub the grill with a soft brass-bristle brush.

Safety. Careless use of a gas grill can lead to a fire or an explosion. You should follow these pointers for safe, trouble-free cookouts:

• Never store a fuel tank indoors. Tanks are designed to vent gas automatically if pressure builds up excessively, as it might on a hot day. LP (liquid petroleum) gas is heavier than air; if it's not dispersed by a breeze, it flows to the lowest point it can reach and collects there. Never permit gas to build up indoors.

• When bringing the tank home after a refill, prop it securely so it can't tip. Drive with a window open.

• Keep the tank upright when you're reconnecting it to the grill's regulator. If it tips, a spurt of the liquid fuel can damage the regulator. Once the tank is attached, check the connection with a few drops of detergent solution; bubbles indicate a leak.

• Clean the grill regularly—once a year or after every 50 cookouts. Clean the burner ports, venturi tubes, and the tip of the igniter. With the gas turned off, check the igniter to be sure it sparks properly.

• Keep the grill well away from combustible surfaces, such as wood siding and deck railings.

• Never use a gas grill in a garage doorway or an enclosed porch, where escaping gas might explode. And don't position the grill under low eaves or overhangs, where the heat might char the wood.

• Use oven mitts and avoid loose-fitting clothing when using the grill.

• If you must buy an extra LP tank, buy only the kind approved by the U.S. Department of Transportation for LP gas. Never buy a used tank, and have any tank inspected professionally every 5 years to make sure that corrosion hasn't caused any leaks.

GENERIC DRUGS

Prescription drugs marketed under their generic names often are half the price of the same drug sold under a brand name—the name given it by the company that held the original patent.

Most generic drugs are manufactured not by fly-by-night

factories but by the very same companies that develop brand-name drugs. In fact, the approximately 60 brand-name drug companies manufacture about 80 percent of all generic drugs as well. Some 300 smaller pharmaceutical companies produce the drugs for the rest of the generic market.

To realize the savings offered by generic drugs, you need the cooperation of both your doctor and your pharmacist. Doctors, for instance, frequently write the brand name when they prescribe drugs. It's shorter and easier to remember than the generic name. And since the brand name had no generic competition during the long life of its patent, the doctor is probably accustomed to writing it.

This medical habit doesn't prevent you from buying generically. The laws in every state allow pharmacists to substitute a less expensive generic version when the doctor prescribes by brand. Indeed, the doctor must make a conscious effort in order to limit you to the brand name. In some states, this means he or she must write out "dispense as written" or some other phrase on the prescription. In other states, the doctor chooses which of two lines on the prescription form to sign. Signing on one line means the patient must receive the brand specified; signing on the other means the pharmacist may substitute a generic drug.

If you switch from a brand name to a generic, the medication's color and shape will be different from the brand-name product you've been taking. The pill's appearance won't affect how the drug works. However, some patients may become confused about medications whose color and/or shape change, particularly if they are in the habit of transferring a day's worth of pills from the prescription vial to a pocket or purse container. An unfamiliar appearance can promote taking the wrong pill at the wrong time and/or in the wrong amount. In such instances, prudence suggests sticking to the brand-name drug, even though it is more expensive.

GLUES

Most glues aren't jacks-of-all-trades. For successful repairs, you need to know their special talents:

Epoxy adhesives come in two parts, a resin and a hardener. These glues are strong, hard, and water-resistant, with fine gap-filling abilities.

Catalyzed acrylic glues are strong, stick to oily surfaces, and can glue almost any material except flexible plastic.

Silicone rubber glues can take a very wide range of temperatures and can be used on most surfaces, but they can't be painted. Their elasticity, water-resistance, and gap-filling properties let them serve as sealants and caulks as well as adhesives.

"Instant" glues, the *cyanoacrylates,* are fast-setting, although they have been reformulated to slow down their bonding speed to a manageable minute or so. The quick bonding is a cyanoacrylate glue's biggest advantage, because it lets you glue hard-to-clamp objects, provided that the mating surfaces are hard and smooth.

Contact cements are flexible adhesives used most often for gluing a plastic laminate to a countertop, resetting a loose wall tile, or reattaching a shoe sole. Their big advantage is that they bond on contact the instant the coated surfaces are brought together (you must first let the glue dry a bit). Because contact cements bond so quickly, they can't be used for gluing joints that must be slid together for final assembly.

Plastic cements are clear adhesives in small squeeze tubes and are commonly used in building model airplanes, model ships, and the like. They shrink as they dry, so they don't work well in loose joints.

White glues are inexpensive, water-based, strong, paintable, and not very flexible. They take a while to harden and can be cleaned up with water before they set.

Aliphatics, also called carpenter's glues, grab faster than white glues, so they require a shorter clamping time. They also shrink less than white glues.

Because of their water-resistance, *resin glues* are often used in construction or marine applications. They are toxic and irritating. Although inconvenient to use, resin glues clasp wood powerfully and resist water well.

You should be able to handle most repairs and do-it-yourself projects with an epoxy glue for very strong bonds on a variety of materials, a white glue or an aliphatic for ease of use and strength on wood, and a cyanoacrylate for quick bonding of hard-to-mend items.

HAIR CONDITIONERS

Advertisers claim that conditioners make hair shine, give it body and bounce, make it soft, make it strong, make it more manageable and tangle-free. Some products claim to provide the protein that hair "craves." Some are supposed to be "self-adjusting," providing as much or as little conditioning as the hair needs.

Conditioners do reduce the roughness of the hair's outer layer, so hair combs easier, looks shinier, and feels softer. By coating each hair, they counteract static electricity, so hair is more manageable. But conditioners that purport to be "self-adjusting" really offer nothing special. Hair takes what it needs and sheds the rest, no matter what brand of conditioner you use.

As for providing extra body for fine hair, any conditioner coats the hair and thus is bound to make each strand slightly thicker. So there's no consistent difference between extra-body and regular varieties of a particular brand.

A conditioner labeled for dry and normal hair usually contains oils or fatty substances, such as mineral oil or lanolin. A formulation labeled for oily hair usually contains "oil free" synthetic polymers, such as silicones, acrylics, and epoxy derivatives. But these special formulations don't seem to have much relationship to how well a conditioner conditions.

A product touted as "nourishing" hair may contain substances such as protein, wheat germ, milk, egg, and honey. But hair, once it is outside the scalp, is not a living thing. It can't be nourished. (A poor diet or poor health, however, can result in poor-looking hair.) Nor can a conditioner permanently repair damaged hair. It may hide split ends temporarily by gluing them together, and protein in the conditioner may even fill in gaps in damaged hair—until you shampoo again. The only way to eliminate damaged hair is to cut it off.

Not everyone needs to condition their hair after shampooing. People with short, healthy hair that has not been color-treated or permed may never need a conditioner. Other people may need to use a conditioner only in the winter, when there's less moisture in the air, or in summer, when exposure to salt water or chlorinated pools may tend to make the hair feel and look dry.

If your hair is more tangled than you think it should be after shampooing, if it tends to be fly-away and unmanageable, or if you'd like it to feel a bit softer or look shinier, it may need more conditioning. If, on the other hand, your hair looks limp and somewhat greasy right after shampooing, you're probably conditioning too much.

HAND AND BATH SOAPS

Don't be taken in by the perfumes, the fancy packaging, and the pretty colors. Soap is merely a cleanser that removes dirt, oily film, and bacteria from your skin—and differences in cleaning effectiveness among soaps are slight.

Soap is actually irritating, not soothing, to the skin. It cleans, and in the process removes the skin's natural oil, drying the skin. In an attempt to make soap less drying, some manufacturers have added extra fats, such as lanolin, moisturizing cream, and cocoa butter. But even super-fatted soap is not a good moisturizer, since it still has a drying effect. A moisturizing lotion applied immediately after bathing works better.

Healthy skin can handle just about any soap. But sensitive or dry skin may fare better with soap that doesn't have added perfume or antiseptics.

HEALTH INFORMATION
The government's National Health Information Clearinghouse (NHIC) will respond to your health questions. NHIC forwards your questions to one or more of the many health-related organizations listed in its database.

To contact the NHIC, call 800-336-4797 (toll free) or 703-522-2590 (in Virginia).

You can also contact some of NHIC's referral organizations directly. Here are a few:

- Alzheimer's Disease and Related Disorders Association
  800-621-0379; 800-572-6037 in Illinois
- National Asthma Center
  800-222-LUNG; 303-398-1477 in Colorado
- National Cocaine Hotline
  800-COC-AINE
- National Abortion Federation
  800-772-9100; 202-546-9060 in Washington, DC
- Pregnancy Crisis Center
  800-368-3336; 804-847-6828 (call collect within Virginia)
- National Parkinson Foundation
  800-327-4545; 800-433-7022 in Florida; 305-547-6666 in Miami
- National Second Surgical Opinion Program Hotline
  800-638-6833; 800-492-6603 in Maryland
- VD National Hotline
  800-227-8922; 800-982-5883 in California

HEATERS: ELECTRIC

A portable electric heater is handy for spot-heating—warming one area quickly. A radiant or radiant/convection unit does this better than a convection-only model, since the reflector in a radiant heater beams the heat directly to objects in its path.

By following a few simple guidelines, you can use the heater and keep warm safely:

• Keep flammables, combustibles, furniture, and curtains away from the heater.

• Make sure the element in a radiant heater is free of flammable material such as dust balls and hair.

• Clean a heater's reflector with a vacuum cleaner (unplug the heater first) to improve its efficiency.

• Keep the heater away from water. If it tips over near water, don't try to right it; first disconnect the power.

• If you need to use an extension cord, be sure it's the kind that can handle 1,500 watts or at least 12 amperes, not the common lamp-type extension cord that's made for lower power demands.

• Don't use an electric heater on the same circuit with another high-wattage appliance, such as a toaster oven.

• Regularly inspect the wall outlet and heater plug and cord for excessive heat. You may need to hire an electrician to take a look at a hot outlet; it could need replacement.

• A heater cord naturally gets warm, so don't cover the cord or leave it coiled or knotted. If the heater has a compartment for cord storage, withdraw the cord fully during use.

• Unplug the heater when it's not in use.

Heating (*see Furnaces*)

HEMORRHOIDS

Most hemorrhoid sufferers, before seeking professional care, try to treat themselves with over-the-counter remedies. Some of the leading products used for this condition contain a number of ingredients, including anesthetics, astringents, counterirritants, and skin protectants, that can make the irritation worse by causing allergic reactions. The worst offenders are the "-caine" anesthetics—benzocaine, dibucaine, and others.

Another anesthetic, pramoxine hydrochloride, differs chemically from the "-caine" anesthetics and seems to cause fewer allergic problems.

Hemorrhoid products are marketed in four basic forms—as cleansers, as suppositories, as creams, and as ointments. *Cleansers* are the best hemorrhoidal product available for keeping the irritated area clean. *Suppositories* often bypass the area that needs treatment, so their effect on hemorrhoids is minimal at best. *Creams* may help to soothe the irritation. *Ointments*, which are greasier, tend to retain moisture, and may encourage itching and irritation. Hydrocortisone, present in several of these products, is an effective anti-itch ingredient. But its overuse may lead to dependency and eventually can cause thinning of the skin.

HOSPICES

A hospice is not a place but a system of care, a way to provide physical and psychological comfort for dying people and their families. Such care differs from traditional hospital care in that the emphasis is on making a dying patient as comfortable and content as possible, not on attempting a cure. Often organized and run by religious or community groups or by hospitals, hospice care usually takes place in the patient's home. However, some hospices are located in homelike units within hospitals or (more rarely) in nursing homes.

You can get the names of hospices near you by phoning a

local cancer information hotline or by asking the discharge planner or community-relations officer at a local hospital. Churches, synagogues, Visiting Nurses Associations, or American Cancer Society offices may also help you to locate a hospice near you.

In making a choice among hospices, you should check into their style of emotional support. Inquire first as to the hospice's orientation: is it secular or religious? Then discuss the hospice's philosophy of pain management, since this is a critical point for the patient as well as for the patient's family. Here are some additional questions that a family should explore:

- Must the patient acknowledge that he or she is terminally ill?
- Will the hospice accept a patient with a diagnosis other than cancer?
- Will the patient be able to continue radiation treatment or chemotherapy if he or she chooses?
- Will the patient keep his or her regular physician?
- Will the patient be able to stay at home for as long as he or she wants to?
- Will hospice personnel teach the family how to feed, bathe, medicate, and otherwise care for the patient?
- Can you use the hospital of your choice?
- What happens if Medicare or insurance coverage runs out? And what would happen if the family's money ran out? Would the patient be cut off from the hospice service?
- Will hospice personnel help sort out and interpret Medicare and insurance policies and bills for the patient and the family?
- Is respite care available to give family members time away from the patient?

- If the patient is a child, does the hospice have the experience to deal with the intensely difficult circumstances surrounding a child's fatal illness?
- Does the hospice provide help and counseling for survivors, and for how long?

HOT DOGS

Americans love hot dogs—they wolf down some 19 billion each year. But this popular fare consists largely of water and fat. Hot dogs are made of odds and ends of meat ground with water and spices; these ingredients are pumped into casings, cooked, cured, and packaged. Currently the U.S. Department of Agriculture (USDA) allows manufacturers to add up to 10 percent more water than is normally found in meat. This water is mostly in the form of ice, which is meant to keep the meat cool while it is being ground.

The USDA also allows manufacturers to make hot dogs with up to 30 percent fat, the amount found in a well-marbled steak. With so much water and fat, there's not much room for protein in a hot dog—it only averages 13 percent, while cooked steak and hamburger are almost 25 percent protein by weight. This means you can pay more for a pound of protein in a hot dog than you would for a pound of protein in a sirloin steak.

Preservatives and Other Ingredients. Processors can also add up to 3.5 percent nonmeat and nonwater ingredients, which are usually binders, such as skim milk. Preservatives and flavorings are also added, including salt; sweeteners, such as corn syrup and dextrose; ascorbic acid (vitamin C) or one of its derivatives, such as sodium erythorbate or sodium ascorbate; and nitrite.

Nitrite is by far the most controversial. It preserves meat and gives it its characteristic color; it also inhibits the growth of the bacterium that causes botulism, a form of food poisoning that's often fatal. The controversy centers on whether nitrite poses a cancer hazard in the quantities consumed. The U.S. Food and Drug Administration and the USDA have permitted the use of lowered amounts of nitrite but have not banned it, mainly because no substitute has been developed that matches its preservative effects. Many scientists also consider any risks posed by nitrite to be minimal, and preferable to the risks of doing without it in cured meats.

Most hot dogs are high in sodium as well: a good-tasting wiener may contain 400 milligrams or more of sodium.

Obviously, hot dogs do not bring joy to the heart of a nutritionist or a prudent dieter. But if you insist on eating them occasionally, buy the best-tasting ones and enjoy them. On an ideal hot dog, the outer "skin" should resist slightly when you bite into it. Breaking through this outer layer, you should be rewarded with a spurt of meaty juice. The meat at the center should be moist and firm.

HOUSEHOLD RECORD-KEEPING

Your current financial papers should all be in one place, easy to get to, and easy to use. When records are no longer current, demote them to a dead-storage file in a closet or the attic. You also need a safe place to keep important papers—a safe-deposit box or, at the least, a fireproof strongbox. A record of how you've arranged your records can also be useful.

You can throw away many records eventually. The rules of the Internal Revenue Service are often the determining factor. The previous three years are fair game for its routine audits (plus "base years" if you income-average); six years, if income was significantly underreported; forever, if fraud is involved.

Keep indefinitely any record related to capital improvements on your home. Their cost reduces the taxable capital gain due when you sell your house and don't reinvest the

HOUSEHOLD RECORD-KEEPING

Document	Where to keep	How long
Canceled checks and bank statements;	Current file	1 year
records of itemized deductions (interest, medical, etc.), and depreciated equipment	Dead storage	5 years
Credit card numbers	Current file	Keep current
Contracts	Safe-deposit box and lawyer	Until expiration
Household inventory	Safe-deposit box and current file	Keep up-to-date
Insurance policies	Current file (policy number in safe-deposit box)	Indefinitely for life insurance; until expiration for others
Loans and promissory notes	Current file	Until paid off
Medical records	Current file	Keep up-to-date
Mortgage records and home-improvement receipts	Safe-deposit box and current file	As long as you own home or roll over profits into new home
Net-worth statements	Current file	Indefinitely
Personal records— birth certificates, marriage and divorce papers, military-service papers	Safe-deposit box	Indefinitely
Real-estate deeds	Safe-deposit box	Until property is sold
Receipts for major purchases	Current file	As long as you own the item
Stock or bond certificates	Safe-deposit box or broker	Until sold

Document	Where to keep	How long
Tax returns	Current file	3 years
	Dead storage	3 years or more
Vehicle titles	Safe-deposit box	Until vehicle is sold or junked
Warranties	Current file	Until expiration
Will	Safe-deposit box and lawyer	Indefinitely

profits in another house—a liability you may face decades from now.

HOUSE PAINTS AND STAINS

For the outside of a house, latex paint is simpler to use than oil-based paint. It's easy to apply and adheres well to damp surfaces. It dries quickly. Spills and spatters as well as tools and hands clean up with plain water.

Oil-based paint (also called alkyd paint) dries faster than it used to—so fast that you can probably apply two coats in as many days. But you still can't apply an alkyd paint to a damp surface, and you still need solvent to clean your hands and everything else after painting.

Paint isn't the only option for sprucing up a home's exterior. Stain offers a mellow, weathered look that may be appropriate on some surfaces, for some styles of house, and in certain settings.

Stain is meant to soak into wood, leaving at most a very thin film on the surface. This is an advantage if you want the texture of the wood to show through the color.

Like paint, stain comes in water- and oil-based formulations. Unlike paint, oil-based stain outsells latex stain. Stain also comes in transparent, semitransparent, and opaque varieties (the last essentially a thin paint).

Paint versus Stain. Most people own a house with existing painted or stained siding made of a natural wood or manufactured wood product such as hardboard or plywood. If the house was stained years ago, the exterior may just look shabby. If it was painted, the exterior may look faded and show signs of cracking and peeling.

Many stain manufacturers advise against using a stain over a painted or otherwise sealed surface. If a stain can't soak into the wood, it may be more difficult to apply, may not cover well, and may erode prematurely.

Latex versus Oil. The convenience of a latex product may tempt you to rule out oil-based paint and stain right from the start. But you should consider the surface you intend to cover. An alkyd product is often the solution to common painting problems.

Peeling and flaking paint is probably the most frequent problem encountered on an exterior surface. Peeling seems to occur most often after several layers of paint have built up or when latex paint has been used over alkyd. Solution: Don't switch formulations. Paint latex over latex, alkyd over alkyd.

Figuring Your Paint Needs. Estimate the distance in feet from the top of the foundation to the eaves (add 2 feet if the roof is pitched) and measure the distance around the foundation. Multiply the two numbers and divide the total by the coverage on the paint can label. That's how many gallons you will need for one coat. You'll need only about half as much for a second coat.

Be sure that all the cans you buy for the job have the same batch number, or the color may vary from can to can.

Tools. Using a roller may seem like a good way to speed up the job. It is. But only a brush will get under the bottom edge of lapped siding or shingles. And only a brush will work the paint into the textured surface of rough-cut shingles. With water-based paints and stains, use a brush with synthetic bristles.

Cleaning. Rent a power washer to save labor in removing eroding or peeling paint or stain and to clean off dirt and grime.

Black speckles on the north side of a house may be dirt, or they may be mildew. Test by spot-cleaning a section with a half-and-half solution of chlorine bleach and water. Mildew will discolor and disappear in minutes. Don't paint or apply stain over mildew, which will pop right through the new surface. Bleach the whole surface and hose off to rinse.

Surface Preparation. Alligatored, checked, blistered, or wrinkled surfaces have to be scraped, wire-brushed, steel-wooled, or sandpapered. Paint won't hide such blemishes.

Repair or replace broken shingles or deteriorated siding. Replace dry, cracked caulk around windows and doors (*see* Caulks: Exterior). Use wood filler or putty to cover nails that can rust. Apply sealer over knotholes and pitch streaks in new wood. Prime those areas as well as any bare wood.

ICE CREAMS

Homemade ice cream is mainly cream, sugar, and natural flavorings, but other ingredients may turn up in commercial products. Stabilizers, for instance, are noted on labels as vegetable gums (guar, locust or carob bean, cellulose). They improve smoothness, minimize growth of ice crystals, and help keep the ice cream from melting rapidly. Emulsifiers (mono- and diglycerides, lecithin, and carrageen) help ice cream hold its smooth emulsion and make it easier to whip air into the mix. And there are others. Many in the ice cream trade defend chemical or processed stabilizers and emulsifiers as necessities. It's interesting to note that certain ice cream makers get along nicely without any of them.

Nutrition. As desserts go, ice cream is not all that fattening. And you get a respectable amount of nutrition along with the calories.

Consider other desserts: a slice of iced yellow cake will add 240 calories; a wedge of apple pie, 410 calories. Have two scoops (one-half cup) of a nonpremium ice cream instead and you get away with about 150 calories on average. More expensive premium ice cream averages about 245 calories a serving. Ice milk runs from 110 to 115 calories a serving.

Like other dairy products, ice cream and ice milk contain a decent amount of protein. A double scoop offers about one-quarter to one-third the protein of an 8-ounce glass of whole or low-fat (1 percent) milk. Yet the average ice cream has about the same number of calories as the whole milk, and the ice milk has roughly the same number of calories as low-fat milk.

Butterfat is the source of half the calories in ice cream. This fat runs some 7 to 8 grams a serving, and it's mainly saturated. If you're watching your fat intake, you're better off with ice milk, which may have only about 3 grams of fat per serving.

After fat, carbohydrates (generally sugars) are the chief source of calories in ice cream. Milk and other dairy products contain sugar naturally. But much of ice cream's sugar has been added.

Storage. However good an ice cream or ice milk tastes at first, it won't taste that good forever. Quality starts to decline after 1 to 4 months following manufacture, even if the ice cream is stored at temperatures below 0°F. When noticeable ice crystals form, the product has started to deteriorate. You could avoid buying stale products if the packages carried a legible manufacturing date. As things stand now, you can't tell what the dates on many packages mean.

To enjoy ice cream at its best, buy it in small quantities. Pick out a rock-hard container of your favorite flavor and have it wrapped separately, preferably in an insulated ice cream bag or in the same bag as other frozen foods. Get it home fast, swathe it in plastic, and put it in the coldest part of the freezer.

IMMUNIZATION FOR ADULTS

Shots and vaccinations aren't just for kids. The U.S. Centers for Disease Control and the American College of Physicians recommend six vaccines for routine use in adults:

• *Tetanus-diphtheria toxoid.* Everyone should obtain a booster shot every 10 years. It is estimated that most adults do not have adequate protection against these two potentially fatal diseases.

• *Rubella vaccine*. Rubella, or German measles, is usually a mild disease in adults, but its effect on a developing fetus can be devastating, producing blindness or other birth defects. The vaccine is recommended for adults who have not previously had rubella or a rubella immunization, especially women of childbearing age. Women contemplating becoming pregnant should check their immunization status, but vaccination for rubella during pregnancy should be avoided.

• *Measles vaccine*. Anyone born after 1956 who did not receive live measles vaccine after 1 year of age should be immunized (unless there's a reliable record of prior infection or laboratory evidence of immunity).

• *Influenza vaccine*. The group at high risk from influenza includes anyone over 65 and adults or children with chronic illnesses, such as heart, lung, kidney, or metabolic disorders (for example, diabetes and cystic fibrosis), chronic anemia, or an impaired immune defense system. An annual flu shot is recommended for anyone in that high-risk group.

• *Pneumococcal vaccine*. Pneumococcal pneumonia affects more than half a million Americans each year, causing at least 25,000 deaths. A single, one-time injection is advised for all older adults, especially those over 65. It's also recommended for patients of any age with chronic heart or lung disease, diabetes, alcoholism, cirrhosis of the liver, Hodgkin's disease, disorders of the spleen, kidney disease, multiple myeloma, cerebrospinal-fluid leaks, sickle-cell anemia, or impaired immune defenses.

• *Hepatitis-B vaccine*. Immunization against hepatitis-B infection, which can cause severe, chronic liver disease, is recommended for people in certain high-risk groups: those who have had household or sexual contact with hepatitis-B carriers, male homosexuals, intravenous drug users, patients and staff of institutions for the mentally retarded, dialysis patients, hemophiliacs, health workers, mortuary staff, and other people who are frequently exposed to blood or blood products.

Since the vaccine is expensive, and previous exposure to the virus may have gone unrecognized, it may be worthwhile to submit a blood specimen for testing. If hepatitis-B antibodies are present, no vaccination is necessary.

INFANTS' SLEEPWEAR

The flame-retardant properties of sleepwear for infants is often preserved during washing by avoiding the use of soap and sticking to detergents only. For best results, follow labeled care directions *exactly*.

INSECT REPELLENTS

Insect repellents don't kill mosquitoes; they just discourage them from biting you. Repellents are usually effective against mosquitoes as well as chiggers, ticks, fleas, and varieties of biting flies. Many protect you against the black fly, whose bite makes a long-lasting wound that can send a victim to the hospital. They don't work against ants or stinging insects like bees or wasps.

An insect repellent can keep you comfortable when you go hiking, picnicking, or camping in infested areas. More important, using a repellent can keep you healthy. Biting pests sometimes carry serious disease—mosquito-borne encephalitis, tick-borne Lyme disease, or Rocky Mountain spotted fever, for example.

The active ingredient in most products is "deet," short for N,N-diethyl-meta-toluamide. Deet is an oily and somewhat sticky liquid. You rub it on your clothing or directly on your body (the parts that are most likely to be exposed to insect attack). But you have to do so knowledgeably. If you use repellent solely on exposed skin, you may actually drive pests to bite you through your unprotected clothing. When trekking into tick-infested areas, treat cuffs, socks, and shoe tops, too.

Repellents are safe on cotton, wool, and nylon. But the chemicals can damage other fabrics, particularly synthetics such as spandex, rayon, and acetate. So be careful about getting any repellent on a bathing suit (often part spandex) or Hawaiian shirts (often rayon). As for polyester or polyester/cotton blends, test the repellent on an inside seam. Damage will show up quickly as softened or discolored material.

The compounds can also mar plastics and painted or varnished surfaces. So be careful about touching plastic eyeglass lenses, wristwatch crystals, auto dashboards, furniture, and the like when you have insect repellent on your hands.

Generally, the higher the concentration of active ingredient, the longer-lasting the protection. But even a 100 percent deet formula may need to be reapplied after an hour or two for protection against voracious bugs such as black flies.

Packaging. *Aerosols* are useful for covering large areas of skin and fabric quickly and with little mess. But even a small can can be several inches tall and weigh more than a half-pound when full—extra bulk you may not want to cram into a backpack. *Pump sprays* are lighter and more compact. *Lotions* generally give you more control over where you apply the repellent than sprays do, and more control over how much you put on. But they may feel somewhat oily or sticky. *Sticks* have a waxy feel but are easy to apply. They're also much less messy than lotions. *Packets* are convenient whether they contain straight lotion or lotion-soaked towelettes.

Precautions. Treat insect repellents with respect. Use them only when necessary and then sparingly, in the weakest strength that does the job. Don't use a repellent on a small child except in a heavily infested area. Even then, use only a product that contains a minimal amount of active ingredients.

We also suggest that you do a "patch test" for possible skin reactions. A day or two before you plan to start using a repellent, apply a small amount to your forearm or thigh. Check the spot for redness over the next 24 to 48 hours. If you find none, you're not likely to have skin problems with that particular formula.

Never spray aerosol or pump products directly on the face. Repellent formulas can harm eyes and cause painful stinging of lips and mucous membranes. Instead, spray into the palm of one hand and use the other hand to apply the liquid on the face. And never spray repellents around lighted cigarettes, campfires, or open flames—repellents are flammable.

INSOMNIA

Occasional sleeplessness doesn't make you a confirmed insomniac. Insomnia has three forms: transient, short-term, and chronic. *Transient* covers occasional episodes of insomnia among normal sleepers, who may suffer a few restless nights because of jet lag, some trouble at the office, or various anxiety-provoking or exciting events. *Short-term* insomnia can come from more serious stress such as job loss, fear of having a serious illness, or a death in the family. *Chronic* insomnia may go on for months or years with no obvious explanation. It may be a symptom of persistent depression, or it may occur with chronic use of sleep medication, too much alcohol, or disturbances of one's "biological clock" (as with someone whose job hours change from time to time).

Various drugs can also promote insomnia. Stimulants such as caffeine and appetite suppressants are well-known offenders. Even some drugs prescribed for insomnia can interfere with normal sleep patterns. Worry about insomnia can make the problem worse.

Any number of common practices can interfere with a good night's sleep. The following measures may help to counter sleep-robbing habits:

- Establish a fixed sleep schedule. Go to bed and get up at set times, and don't try to make up for lost sleep on weekends and holidays.
- Stop napping, day or evening.
- Never stay in bed when you can't sleep. Do something you find relaxing—read, listen to music, watch television—until you're sleepy.
- Exercise regularly, preferably in the morning or well before dinner.
- Avoid caffeine in the late afternoon or evening.
- Eat at the same time each day, and try to plan evening activities that are conducive to relaxation, including light exercise such as a leisurely walk.
- Minimize external distractions that may disturb you at bedtime. For example, use dark window shades or eye coverings to block out annoying light.

If insomnia persists despite sleep-hygiene measures, it's time for professional help, especially if the problem is disrupting your life. An internist or other primary-care physician is a good first choice. But a brief visit and a prescription for sleep medication may be a sign that you are not getting the help you need. A caring physician will spend time taking a thorough medical history, including a sleep history. Depending on the problem, the prescription may range from a full-scale medical exam to a short course of medication or a referral to a sleep clinic.

IODINE AND NUTRITION

Iodized salt is often believed to be an important source of iodine, and is therefore a matter of some concern to people who are on low-sodium diets.

Dietary iodine deficiency, once prevalent in the Middle West and Northwest, is far less likely to occur nowadays, even without the use of iodized salt. A significant amount of iodine in the U.S. diet now comes from the residue of iodine-containing substances used in food processing. Dairy farmers, for example, use such chemicals to disinfect and sanitize equipment and often add iodine to cattle feed to prevent goiter in their cows. As a result, milk and other dairy products provide about half of the iodine in the American diet. Seafood and bread are also excellent sources. Accordingly, you can skip iodized salt entirely and still get ample amounts of iodine on a low-sodium diet.

IRONS: STEAM

Before you get a fancy, modern iron, consider what you iron. If you use an iron just now and then, perhaps all you need is a plain steam iron. Chances are, however, that ironing chores will be a bit easier if you get an iron with more features.

Three types of persons should consider paying for an iron with extras: those who iron everything from cotton to acetate; those who are as apt to press in wrinkles as press them out; and those who want a steam iron that shuts off automatically.

Features. Here are some features to look for:

• *Spray and burst of steam.* A built-in spray wets down a little patch in front of the iron; a burst of steam at the press of a button lets you set creases or smooth stubborn wrinkles. Both features are useful for dealing with the sort of wrinkles that crop up in clothing made of natural fibers.

• *Automatic shutoff.* This useful device is typically connected with indicator lights. The simplest design has a small light that shines steadily while the iron is on. If you leave the iron upright for about 15 minutes or in the ironing position for half a minute without moving it, the light flashes and the iron shuts off. Another design has three lights—an amber light that glows while the iron is plugged in, a red Wait light that comes on when the iron is heating or cooling, and a green Ready light that comes on when the iron reaches the selected temperature. This iron shuts off after 10 minutes upright or about 30 seconds without movement while in the ironing position.

• *Temperature control.* Look for a control that's clearly marked and located on the front of the handle, where you can adjust it with one hand. A control that's under the handle is hard to see and takes two hands to adjust.

• *Control buttons.* Look for clearly marked controls that can be easily operated with one hand. The best steam/dry controls are on the front of the iron. Many irons have the button awkwardly placed on the side. The best spray/burst-of-steam controls don't interfere with each other.

• *Fabric guide.* If you don't iron often, look for a guide that gives temperature settings for a variety of fabrics.

• *Cord (while ironing).* Try the iron first to see if the cord hits your wrist. The best design sends the cord off to the side. You can switch the cord from side to side on a few models.

• *Water gauge.* Look for a see-through plastic water chamber. Very dark plastic tanks are nearly impossible to see through, although they do hide unsightly mineral accumulations.

• *Button groove.* Look for a groove that extends along the side of the soleplate. If there are only short notches, they may be shallow and ineffective.

• *Weight.* Some people prefer a heavy iron, while others say a light iron is easier on the arm. Balance is probably more important than actual weight. Before you buy, pick the iron up and pretend to use it. It should feel well balanced and comfortable in your hand.

• *Cordless irons.* These appliances have been on the market, on and off, for more than half a century, but the technology hasn't improved noticeably. These irons heat up in a separate base, which is what is plugged into the electrical outlet. In order to keep the iron hot, the cordless iron has to be set into its base often. This can be a nuisance—more of a nuisance than a trailing electric cord.

Maintaining an Iron. Past experience may have taught you to use distilled water to avoid clogging an iron's steam vents with minerals. But most manufacturers today say that unless you have extremely hard water—more than 180 parts per million of dissolved minerals—ordinary tap water is fine. Water that's been run through a water softener still has minerals in it, and should be considered in the same category as hard water—at least for use in an iron.

Some irons have a removable soleplate. This lets you clean out accumulated minerals that might otherwise stain clothes. On a model with a burst-of-steam feature, you can use the burst to dislodge debris and mineral residue from the steam vents. If an iron lacks any special cleaning features, the best you can do is to fill the iron, set it on High, and iron over an old all-cotton towel for several minutes. Another way to help prevent a buildup of minerals is to empty the iron of water before storing it.

Nonstick soleplates are easy to clean, but be careful about ironing over metal zippers and snaps, which can scratch the nonstick coating.

An iron draws a lot of current. To avoid blowing a fuse or tripping a circuit breaker, don't plug one into the same circuit where another heating appliance (such as a toaster or toaster oven) is operating. If you can't set up the ironing board next to an outlet, use a heavy-duty extension cord.

IRONS: TRAVEL IRONS AND STEAMERS
An old, reliable method of smoothing rumpled clothes when you're away from home is to hang them in the bathroom and

turn on a hot shower. The warm steam relaxes superficial wrinkles. Portable steamers are an extension of this idea, with an important improvement: you can aim the steam. And a steamer is easier to use than an iron—you can remove wrinkles without taking clothes off the hanger simply by moving the steamer up, down, and sideways over each item.

While steamers may be all right for touch-ups, they can't set a crease in trousers or put the crisp pleat back in a cotton skirt. Creases require heat and some pressure. For clothes that need to be pressed, a miniature iron works better than a steamer.

A small travel iron, however, doesn't get as hot or steam as much as a full-size iron. It's also lighter, has a smaller soleplate or ironing surface, holds less water, and offers fewer features than a regular iron. And any iron, regardless of size, is clumsy to use on a hotel desk top padded with a towel.

Steamers and travel irons are make-do appliances. A traveler faced with a badly wrinkled suit would probably be better off using a hotel's valet service or a nearby dry cleaner. But a steamer or a travel iron may do just fine for touch-ups.

If you select a wardrobe carefully, pack judiciously, and unpack promptly, you may avoid wrinkled clothes altogether. In a pinch, you can always try the shower trick.

KEROSENE HEATERS

A kerosene heater should be used cautiously and prudently, if at all. If you insist on buying one, look for a brand that protects you against fire and burn hazards by providing guards or grilles around the heater, a manual shut-off device, and a wick-stop mechanism.

No unvented kerosene heater can be relied on to burn cleanly enough to ease concerns about indoor air pollution. Pollution levels are directly related to the size of the space being heated and to the way the space is ventilated. If you must use an unvented kerosene heater, keep the door to the room open and allow for still more air circulation by opening a window at least a crack.

LADDERS: EXTENSION

An extension ladder is essentially two ladders combined. One, the base section, rests on the ground. The other, the fly section, slides up and down; typically, it's moved with a rope and pulley. Locks on one of the fly section's rungs keep the ladder extended.

The lengths considered most suitable for household use are 16 to 24 feet, although longer ladders are available.

The duty ratings are Type I (industrial), rated at a 250-pound load; Type II (commercial), 225 pounds; and Type III (household), 200 pounds. These loads indicate the maximum weight of climber and equipment that should be put on the ladder in normal use. Be sure to set the ladder at the proper angle against the wall. The recommended angle is 75.5°. Newer ladders have a diagram on their side to help you estimate that angle.

A ladder that conforms to the requirements of Underwriters Laboratories (UL) and the American National Standards Institute (ANSI) is labeled to indicate that it meets the duty-rating standard.

LADDERS: FOLDING

A folding ladder can be unfolded into an A shape to work as a stepladder or into an inverted U to act as a small scaffold.

It can be made to kneel on a staircase, stand off from a wall, become a worktable trestle, or even stand straight like an ordinary ladder. It also folds into a compact, easily transported package. Despite these conveniences, a standard extension ladder or stepladder is more comfortable to stand on for extended work sessions, and extension ladders are available with a much higher reach. Nevertheless, a folding ladder has unbeatable versatility and can be a useful adjunct in many workshops.

When you use a folding ladder as a scaffold, lay a plank along the rungs to act as a catwalk. This distributes the load over several rungs, is easier on the hinges, and reduces bowing in the middle.

The rungs on most folding ladders aren't very comfortable, because they aren't as deep as the rungs on conventional stepladders or extension ladders.

The locking tabs on a folding ladder's hinges can pinch your fingers if you're not careful. You also have to be careful about finger-pinching when you fold some models for storage, if the sections lie flat against each other.

LATEX INTERIOR PAINTS

Most paints seem to go a lot farther than the manufacturers say they will, but this doesn't mean you'll be able to paint more wall for the money. When paint is applied at its natural spreading rate with a roller, the coat is thinner. Therefore, more coats are needed for adequate coverage. Trying to apply a thicker coat usually leads to drips and sags, as well as to a tendency to smear the paint on the wall.

If you're refreshing a canary yellow room with a new coat of canary yellow, you stand a good chance of doing the job in one coat no matter what brand of paint you use. But if you're going from a white room to a pastel, or from one pastel to another, you're likely to need two coats to hide the old

color. With some paints and some colors, you may need three
coats—or even more.

LAUNDERING
When filling a clothes washer, you can save some bother, and
some money on hot water, with a simple approach that still
gives a clean wash. Sort out the obviously troublesome items—
oily overalls and brand-new blue jeans. Then wash everything
else together in warm or cold water. If clothes aren't heavily
soiled, and your laundry needs freshening more than scouring, you'll probably lose nothing in cleaning. And you'll have
spared yourself the traditional chore of sorting whites from
colored items and cottons from synthetics, washing some items
in hot water, bleaching some things, and so forth.

However, you may still want to do a special load now and
then. To do a load that's all colorfast cottons, for instance,
use a hot wash/cold rinse; if the dirt is really bad, first let the
load soak awhile. If you use bleach, use liquid chlorine bleach,
which can whiten twice as well as oxygen "all-fabric" bleaches.
But don't use chlorine bleach on wool, silk, mohair, or items
that aren't colorfast.

LAUNDRY BLEACH
There's more than one kind of bleach. Which is the best to
use? Both chlorine and nonchlorine bleaches use an oxidizing
agent (usually sodium hypochlorite or sodium perborate) that
reacts with and, with the help of a detergent, lifts out a stain.
Chlorine bleach whitens best, but all-fabric powdered bleach
has the advantage of being safe with most fabrics and dyes,
even over long-term use. However, they're a lot more expensive to use than chlorine bleach, and aren't as good at whitening.

You can get extra whitening performance out of powdered
all-fabric bleaches, if you prefer them. If you double the rec-

ommended dose, a good all-fabric bleach approaches chlorine bleach in whitening ability.

LAUNDRY DETERGENTS

A large number of detergents compete for your washday dollar. The differences among them, however, are fairly minor. The dirt dissolvers in synthetic detergents are soaplike molecules (surfactants) that emulsify oil and grease and the dirt they attract and hold, allowing them to be washed away.

So-called *anionic* surfactants are used most widely. These molecules are especially effective at cleaning clay and mud from cotton and other natural fibers. The hotter the water, the better they work. Like soap, synthetic anionics don't work that well in hard water, so they are often combined with water-softening compounds such as phosphates.

Nonionic surfactants are much less sensitive to hardness in water, and the switch to nonphosphate formulas has boosted their use. Nonionics are particularly effective at cleaning oily soil from polyester and other synthetics in cool-wash temperatures. Many liquid detergents are based on surfactants of this type.

Cationic surfactants are found less commonly in detergents than in fabric softeners. Their use will probably increase as manufacturers develop more products combining detergents and softeners.

Anionic surfactants are high-sudsing; nonionic surfactants, low-sudsing. The amount of suds does matter in a front-loading washing machine, where an excess can overflow or interfere with the washing process. In a top-loading washing machine, the amount of suds has no connection with a detergent's cleaning power.

Phosphates. Phosphates are used in detergents to build up the performance of the surfactants by softening the water, dispersing dirt, and emulsifying greasy soil. These important chemicals have an unfortunate negative effect: they hasten the transformation of lakes into swamps in a process called eutrophication. Consequently, they have been banned for nearly 20 years in a number of places, to the point where they are unavailable to about 30 percent of the population, especially in states around the Great Lakes and Chesapeake Bay.

The absence of phosphates does affect the cleaning ability of detergents, so some manufacturers often make a phosphate and a nonphosphate version of the same powder brand and sell the one appropriate to the region. Nonphosphate powders typically use old-fashioned washing soda, with some extra ingredients to make up for the lack of phosphates.

Enzymes. Liquid detergents are probably an outgrowth of the restrictions on phosphates. The liquids are phosphate-free, largely because phosphates aren't very stable in liquid form. The cleaning power of liquid detergents is helped along by enzymes, which make otherwise insoluble stains easy to wash away. These substances actually "digest" stains on clothes. The use of enzymes is increasing as phosphates disappear and wash temperatures grow colder.

Dyes and Other Agents. Most detergents contain colorless, water-soluble dyes known as fluorescent whiteners or optical brighteners. The dyes convert some of the invisible ultraviolet light from the sun or fluorescent lights into visible light, which gives fabrics a "glow." The effect doesn't work as well under incandescent light, so garments washed in a detergent containing a lot of whiteners may look drab in normal household lighting.

Laundry detergents also contain special "antiredeposition" agents to keep dirt in suspension until it's rinsed away. Since even the best of these agents can't cope with lots of dirt, manufacturers will instruct you to wash heavily soiled items separately.

Washing Ability. Differences between the best and worst

detergents may be noticeable but they aren't *very* noticeable. The scale is really from clean to cleanest rather than from dirty to clean.

Fabrics. Synthetics hold on to stains more tenaciously than cotton and other natural fibers. And detergents behave differently on polyester and nylon, whose chemistries differ greatly. Polyester attracts oil, for instance, while nylon resists it. Nylon, however, tends to pick up colors from other items in the wash. The lesson to be learned is that experimental switching from one detergent to another may help to solve some of your nagging laundering problems.

Safety. The chemicals in any detergent can irritate eyes, mucous membranes, or sensitive skin. Like any cleaning product, detergents should be used with commonsense care and kept out of the reach of young children. It's also a good idea to avoid prolonged contact with products that are extremely alkaline or that contain enzymes.

Some people have complained of skin rashes caused by one or another laundry product. While they aren't uncommon, such symptoms are generally not serious, and they disappear quickly when the irritant is removed. If you suspect a laundry product of causing rashes or other such problems, stop using it and see if the symptoms subside.

LAWN MOWERS

In shopping for a lawn mower, you have several decisions to make: Should the mower be powered by gasoline, electricity, or muscle power? Should it be a push-it-yourself, self-propelled, or riding model?

Power. Electric mowers are light, quiet, and easy to start, but their cord makes them awkward to use. Most people choose a gasoline model for its power and mobility. Some have a two-cycle engine, which uses a mixture of gasoline and oil for both fuel and lubricant. But most have a more convenient four-cycle engine, which runs on straight gasoline and has a separate oil reservoir.

Gasoline mowers can be hard to start, but this is often because of an awkwardly placed starter cord that takes an inordinate effort to pull. *Any* gasoline mower can become hard to start if it isn't properly serviced on a regular basis. Gasoline mowers are also noisy enough to be a nuisance, though probably not enough to damage your hearing.

Gasoline Rotary. A gasoline-powered rotary lawn mower is the kind to buy for a medium-size lawn that's fairly flat and without hard-to-mow areas. For a larger lawn, consider a self-propelled, gasoline-powered unit. Mowers with an engine that keeps running when you stop the blade are best for convenience.

If you usually bag clippings, a rear-bagger is your best bet—it holds more clippings than a mower whose bag protrudes to one side, and it lets you cut close to obstructions on either side of the mower. But if you don't use a grass bag, a side-discharge mower generally disperses clippings better than a rear-bagger does. With a side-discharge mower, however, you can't cut close to trees or flower beds from the right side—the discharge chute interferes.

Most side-discharge mowers, however, offer a major inconvenience. They include a type of safety control that turns the engine off whenever you let go of the handle. You can buy an electric starter for some models, but that adds $50 to $100 to the price.

Electric Rotary. Electric mowers have two serious drawbacks. They go only as far as their cord, so they are limited to small lawns. (Mowing more than about one-quarter of an acre requires too much cord to manage easily.) At that, an electric mower may make you cope with a hundred feet or more of cord snaked across the lawn.

To deal with the electric-cord problem, you can coil the

cord and mow back and forth, moving farther from the coil with each pass. Some mowers automatically keep the cord out of the way through a turn.

Riding Mower. These machines cut a swath 2 to 4 feet wide. They're for homeowners with more than half an acre of lawn. The biggest models are tiny tractors that can be outfitted with attachments that plow snow, spread seed, and the like.

The odds of being injured with a riding mower are higher than with a walk-behind model. All new riding mowers have some important safety features—an interlock that prevents the engine from starting when the mower is in gear or the blade is engaged, a blade that stops quickly when you disengage it, and a "deadman" control that stops the blade automatically if you fall off or climb off the seat.

Reel Mower. For very small lawns, you may want to consider a hand-powered reel mower. Reel mowers are small, lightweight, and very quiet. However, they can't handle grass or weeds more than 3 or 4 inches tall, and they can't trim as close to a fence or a wall as most rotary models. If you set a reel to cut grass short (which is a good setting for low-growing grasses such as Bermuda and bent grass), you run the risk of scalping the lawn, particularly on rough, uneven ground.

LIFE INSURANCE

There are huge differences among life insurance policies. Here's how to sort out what you need:

Estimating Insurance Needs. Don't depend on an agent to figure out how much insurance you need. Do that yourself, using the worksheet on page 146. You need to consider your family's future expenses, including child care and college costs, and your family's current assets. Don't be surprised if the calculation reveals that you may need $100,000 to $200,000 or more in life insurance coverage.

WORKSHEET: HOW MUCH LIFE INSURANCE DO YOU NEED?

What you need

Immediate expenses
  Federal estate taxes $_____
  State inheritance taxes   _____
  Probate costs   _____
  Funeral costs   _____
  Uninsured medical costs   _____
    Total final expenses $_____
Future expenses
  Family expense fund   _____
  Emergency fund   _____
  Child care expenses   _____
  Education fund   _____
  Repayment of debts   _____
    Total future expenses $_____
      Total needs $_____

What you have now

Cash and savings   _____
Equity in real estate   _____
Securities   _____
IRA and Keogh plans   _____
Employer savings plans [e.g., 401(k)]   _____
Lump-sum employer pension benefits   _____
Current life insurance   _____
Other assets   _____
  Total assets $_____

Extra insurance needed

(*Total needs minus total assets*)
Total needs $_____
Total assets $_____
  Additional insurance needed $_____

Affordable Insurance. The three basic types of life insurance are term, whole life, and universal life. For most families, *term* insurance will provide the greatest coverage for the lowest cost. At the time of purchase and for many years afterward, term premiums are the least expensive. *Whole life* premiums are generally the most expensive. Premiums for *universal life* policies are often lower than whole life premiums but still higher than term premiums.

Term premiums do rise as you get older and the cost of providing insurance protection increases, but they usually don't reach the level of whole life premiums for many years. By that time you may need relatively little insurance coverage—or perhaps none at all.

Some insurance agents know that whole life or universal life is too expensive for most people, so they often suggest a combination of term and either whole life or universal. It's best to avoid these combination plans. They're a way for the company to hook you to the "permanent" type of coverage it really wants to sell.

Term insurance is perfectly respectable. It is not "poor man's coverage," as some agents would lead you to believe.

Insurance as Savings. A life insurance policy is not a very liquid investment. You can get locked into either a universal life or a whole life policy for several years because the start-up costs of these types of policies are high.

But universal life policies appear to have better rates of return in the early years than whole life policies. Furthermore, a universal life policy has more flexibility. But the flexibility of its elements requires that you pay attention to all notices and statements from the insurance company so you'll know if the policy is in danger of lapsing.

Dividend-paying Insurance. A policy that pays dividends is called *participating*. Insurance policy dividends are a partial return of the premiums you've paid. Premiums for a participating policy are generally higher than for a nonparticipating one.

If you buy term insurance, dividends are likely to be small, so it hardly matters whether the policy is participating or nonparticipating.

Practically speaking, a universal life policy is priced to pay no dividends, so the dividend issue is important mainly if you buy whole life. A participating whole life policy is likely to be a better buy than the nonparticipating variety.

Which Company? Insurance companies do sometimes go bankrupt, but state insurance regulators usually get another company to take over. Nevertheless, such a bankruptcy could cause you red tape and delay at best, reduced dividends or cash value at worst.

Unless you have independent knowledge of a company's financial condition, buy from a company rated A+ or A for financial stability by *Best's Insurance Reports,* a reference book available in many libraries.

Comparison Shopping. Ask three or four agents to present one or more policies of the type you want. Compare *interest-adjusted net cost indexes* (if it's a term or a whole life policy). The lower the index, the less costly the policy. If an agent refuses to give you the index, go to another.

Keep in mind that bigger doesn't necessarily mean better. Some of the best life insurance buys are from small or medium-size companies.

The Agent. If you find an agent who is attentive to your needs, explains policy details clearly, and puts your family's interests ahead of his or her commission income, you may be willing to pay a little more for a policy to keep his or her services. Service may be especially important with universal life. A good agent will contact you periodically to see whether the policy still meets your needs and whether you should consider any adjustments in premiums or in the amount of coverage.

LIPSTICKS

No one lipstick has all the qualities you may want. A long-lasting lipstick may appear to change color over time. A very creamy lipstick may slide on easily, but it will tend to feather and won't stay put. A waxy lipstick won't moisturize well. You'll have to decide which factor is most important to you and compromise on the others.

Here are a few lipstick qualities judged important by a professional makeup artist:

Application. How easy a lipstick is to put on depends on how it's packaged, how opaque it is, how easily it spreads, and whether or not it smears. A creamy or opaque lipstick is usually easier to apply than one that's waxy or sheer (lacking in opacity).

Creaminess. Creamy lipsticks glide on smoothly and moisturize lips, but they can smear and bleed. Creaminess and waxiness are usually at odds with one another.

Opacity. With an opaque lipstick, you needn't apply a thick layer to get the color you want, and, chances are, the color on your lips will match the color in the tube. However, opaque lipsticks, especially glossy ones, can make lips look painted and less natural than sheer lipsticks.

Gloss. Glossy lipsticks give lips a shiny, wet look. But both glossy and frosted lipsticks reflect light and thus tend to accentuate flaws. If your lips are wrinkled or chapped, you'll do better with a lipstick that has a matte finish.

Blotting Resistance. The price you pay for a lipstick that doesn't come off on a coffee cup is that it may not come off when you want it to. Creamy lipsticks normally blot off more quickly than waxy ones.

Removal. Normally, a lipstick that's easy to put on is also likely to be easier to take off.

Staining. Lipsticks that contain a relatively high concentration of dye can stain your lips. They'll also stay on your lips longer—though the color may change as the less permanent pigments wear off. Don't assume that a lighter lipstick color won't stain.

Color. The shades you choose to wear should match your skin tone. If you have yellowish or olive skin, peaches, corals, "warm" pinks, and orange-reds will look best. People whose skin has a blue undertone look good in clear reds and shades of pink.

Tips on Application

• Use a brush. This is especially important for bright, opaque lipsticks, where precise control is critical.

• Use a lip liner to help define your lips and keep the color from feathering beyond the lip line. When you use pale, natural shades of lipstick, the liner should match your own lip color as closely as possible. With brighter shades, match the liner to the lipstick.

• Blot, reapply, and powder to make lipstick last for several hours. Do this two or three times, then finish with a light dusting of face powder to set the lipstick.

LONG-DISTANCE TELEPHONING

Under the equal-access program, you must choose one long-distance firm as your primary carrier. If you don't, your local phone company will assign one to you. (Equal access may not apply to your area yet.)

You are not obliged to use your chosen company for *all* of your long-distance calls. Instead, you can make calls with any company serving your area by dialing a five-digit code (which you can get by calling the "800" number of the company whose service you want to use).

The clarity of the connection and the absence of echoes or voice delays can be important elements in determining your satisfaction with a long-distance company. However, voice quality depends on many factors, several of which are determined by the local phone company rather than by the long-distance carrier. If you routinely call a particular long-distance number or a particular city (and you already have equal access), the best way to compare voice quality is to do your own tests. Switch among the competing carriers by using their five-digit codes. Try this several times to see if you can spot a consistent trend in voice quality.

LUGGAGE: CARRY-ON

The bag you carry onto an airplane is the one you don't have to wait for later at the luggage pickup. If an airplane doesn't have much underseat room, a soft or semisoft bag has an advantage because it can be forced into place, adjusting to the available space. Here's what to look for in soft luggage:

Handles. A good design includes two strap handles that can be joined together by a wraparound flap secured by snaps or Velcro. The width of the flap is more important than the material of which it's made: A flap that isn't as wide as your palm may dig into your hand. A flap that doesn't easily wrap around the handles quickly becomes a bother to use.

Strap handles that can't be joined with a flap fall to the sides of the bag when you put it down. Every time you pick up the bag, you have to gather up the straps—a nuisance.

Rigid-frame bags and some semisoft bags have a conventional suitcase handle. The most comfortable handles of that type have padding on the underside.

Shoulder Straps. When your hands are occupied with tickets, reading material, and other paraphernalia, a bag with a shoulder strap is a boon. Since the strap itself may be narrow, look for the type that has a shoulder pad with a textured surface that provides friction so the strap doesn't slip from your shoulder.

A shoulder strap should be removable for occasions when you don't need it.

Floor. A floor helps to distribute the weight of a bag's contents. A soft floor, without any stiffening, is not very effective. A floor attached to the bag on one side only can be tipped up to let the bag collapse for storage.

Compartments. A handy design features a wide center compartment flanked by narrower ones. Pockets that don't run the full width of a bag are for stowing miscellaneous items: a plastic-lined pocket is handy for carrying a damp swimsuit. Zippers or snap-tabs on pockets help keep things in place. Exterior pockets should have a zipper or a secure latch, because it's the outside pocket you may want to use for stowing those important items you need quick access to, such as airline tickets and medications.

Straps and Hangers. Look for tie-down straps to keep clothes folded and in place. They should be long enough to go around clothing and also be easy to drape out of the way when you are packing.

Zippers. Plastic zippers operate much more smoothly than metal ones. Double-pull zippers should go around three sides of a bag. This lets you open just one side of the bag to fish something out or unzip the bag all the way for convenient packing and unpacking.

Style and Appearance. That's a matter of individual taste. But keep in mind that a light-colored bag will show dirt, and a bag of a dark color will develop a whitish haze caused by abrasion. Medium-intensity colors are probably best. Tweeds also hide dirt well.

LUGGAGE: SOFT-SIDED

Soft. The protectiveness of a piece of luggage depends largely on its framing. There are three categories of framing: soft, partial-frame, and full-frame. The construction of soft-sided luggage covers a broad range. At one end are bags without any stiffness at all. They protect their contents the least, but offer a good deal of adaptability in stowing oddly shaped items, and they're fine for jeans, socks, shoes, and casual clothing. They're also very easy to store and can be pummeled—within reason—into tight storage spots when fully packed.

Partial-frame. Only slightly more protective is "partial-frame" luggage. Some of these bags have a stiff bottom panel and merely a suggestion of a frame—springy wires encased in bindings around the edge. Others have a narrow steel band around their middle that supports the handle. Empty, a bag with a partial frame can be folded fairly flat for storage. Like a soft bag, however, it leaves it to your cargo to expand the bag to its full width, so it's a bit awkward to pack and none too convenient if you have to live out of a suitcase. And its design protects it only at limited points against the squashing and bangs met with in the cargo hold of an airplane.

Full-frame. As soft-sided luggage goes, a bag with full-width framing gives the best protection against rough handling. Where a partial-width frame gives a bag a stable shape in length and height, a "full" frame gives a bag shape and protectiveness in width as well.

A full-frame soft-sided bag isn't necessarily stiff, however. Its frame can range from a plastic flexibility to a steely rigidity. Nor is the full-frame effect necessarily caused by a full frame. In some luggage, the frame is a band some 6 to 8 inches wide protecting the full width of the bag. But in others, the frame is about 2 inches wide, with prominent plastic inserts at the corners that hold the bag square. This design can make a bag hard to close—you must tug and pull the lid over the inserts.

Because a full-frame bag holds its shape like a dresser drawer, it's relatively convenient to pack and live out of, if necessary. But by the same token, such a bag demands the same space whether full, partly full, or empty—a consideration if you have limited storage space.

You can do a quick in-store check of a soft-sider's rigidity by pressing firmly, then releasing, the bag's top, sides, and corners. The less they yield and the faster they rebound, the more protection they're likely to offer. Note that even the most rigid full-frame case isn't firm enough to be sat on or stepped on when empty or when full, especially the edges.

Wheels. If much of your traveling is done on public transportation, wheels on a suitcase can save you undue exertion. Most wheeled bags have two swiveling wheels at the front and a fixed pair at the rear.

A four-wheel case trails you like a reluctant dog, usually pulling your arm straight behind you. A two-wheeled case trundles along at your side when you lift up the front end. It takes some extra effort to keep it upended as you proceed.

With wheels an inch or less in diameter, a four-wheel bag has a tiny "footprint" that impedes the bag's progress on carpeting and rough surfaces. Bigger (2-inch) wheels on a two-wheeler make it easier to roll the bag along pebbly surfaces. But any wheeled bag should do well on a smooth straightaway.

Handles. The handles on a suitcase are usually one of two basic varieties: top-mounted or side-attached. A top-mounted handle is most often a single grip—sometimes a U-shaped piece of molded plastic with a bit of cushioning, sometimes a single or double strap or a strap with a row of stitching down the middle that gives it the look of twin tubes. The dimensions vary, and any handle should provide enough clearance for your gloved hand.

Handles attached at the sides are twin looped straps like those on a shopping bag, some with a small cover that snaps over the paired straps as cushioning. If you are short, check to make sure you can lift and carry the bag without holding your arm at a tiring angle.

Watch out for zippers that are secured by easy-to-unravel chain stitching. Avoid weak attachments for components and sharp rivets on the inside. Check all hardware and interior fittings for proper function and secure attachment.

MAIL-ORDER FOODS

The high prices charged by mail-order food companies often buy you fancy packaging and trimmings: filet mignon may be delivered in a Styrofoam cooler packed with dry ice; fruit comes wrapped in tissue paper and foil and packed in a carton stuffed with protective "grass." But do fancy prices buy better quality than you can get from a local store?

Filet Mignon. Most people who buy mail-order steak buy it as a gift for someone else. The best mail-order steaks are tender and flavorful, with no off-flavors or visible fat or gristle. But consumers who order by mail for themselves, assuming they are getting a superior product, should first check out a local butcher shop. Prime filet mignon could turn out to be as good there as the best mail-order steak, and a lot less expensive.

Smoked Salmon. If you're buying mail-order salmon as a gift, don't expect top quality. Buy the least expensive brand you can, and hope the fancy wrapping pleases the gift's recipient enough to compensate for what's inside. If you're buying for yourself, you may get better salmon by shopping around the corner.

Cheddar Cheese. You may find a good, fresh cheddar locally, one as good as the best you can get by mail. Look for cheese that's creamy yellow, with no color change or dryness at the edges. There should be a slight crumbliness at the cut edge, and the cheese should be wrapped tightly.

Coffee Beans. Coffee beans are an ideal mail-order food. They require no special packaging or handling and they're not heavy. An unusual variety of coffee can be a nice present for someone who doesn't have a specialty shop nearby. And it can be fun for yourself, since you can experiment conveniently with various types that may not be available in your area.

In most cases, it should take a week or two for a mail-order company to deliver your order. If the package spoils during shipping or the person you sent it to is not satisfied when it arrives, most mail-order companies will refund your money or reship the order.

MAIL-ORDER FRAUD
Here are a few tips to help you avoid becoming a fraud victim:

• Read advertisements carefully and completely, especially the fine print. Don't rely on pictures and headlines.
• Never send cash. Pay by check, money order, or credit card so you have a receipt of payment.
• Don't send for a product from a company you're not familiar with if the advertisement lists only a post-office box. It's possible that the company doesn't want anyone to know its exact location.
• Don't order from companies that *require* the use of toll-free "800" numbers and charge cards. This may be an attempt to avoid use of the mails and thus get around federal postal laws.
• Beware of high-pressure tactics. Don't fall for "can't miss" deals, "last time" offers, "once in a lifetime" opportunities, and "limited supply" sales. Take your time and make an unpressured decision.

• Keep all advertisements, envelopes, and correspondence from a company in case you have complaints about your order. (Some firms require that you send in the original ad with your order. In that case, photocopy the ad before sending it in.) If you order by phone, make a record of the order—price, time, and date of your conversation, and the name of the person you talked with.

MAIL-ORDER PROBLEMS

Even the best mail-order company can make a mistake. Most will act quickly to settle a problem, but some may not.

If you run into trouble, write a letter to the company explaining what went wrong with your order. If you telephone to complain, write a follow-up letter. If you don't hear in 30 days, write to these other agencies:

• *Direct Marketing Association (DMA),* 6 E. 43rd St., New York, NY 10017, 212-689-4977. The DMA sponsors a Mail Order Action Line that will intervene with companies on your behalf and/or refer you to other agencies. If you want your name removed from national mailing lists, write the DMA's Mail Preference Service at the address above. To have your name removed from telephone-sales lists, write the DMA's Telephone Preference Service.

• *Better Business Bureau (BBB),* Council of Better Business Bureaus Inc., 1515 Wilson Blvd., Arlington, VA 22209, 703-276-0100. The BBB can help you check a company's record and reputation before you place an order, and it accepts complaints if you've already ordered and have a problem. You must contact the BBB office nearest the company's headquarters, not the office in your area. To get a directory of BBB offices, contact the council at the address above.

• *Federal Trade Commission (FTC),* Pennsylvania Ave. and 6th St., N.W., Washington, DC 20580, 202-326-2180. The FTC does not act on individual complaints, but it does use them to build cases against fraudulent or nonresponsive companies.

- *State and local consumer-protection agencies.* Agencies in your area may also be able to help resolve your problem.

MATTRESS SETS

Over time, any mattress that's used regularly will show signs of wear. Familiar symptoms include broken springs, frayed or torn ticking, sagging edges, and permanent indentations in the hip or shoulder area. How long a mattress set (mattress and box spring) lasts depends on how much use and abuse it gets, and on whether it is periodically turned and rotated.

The typical 15-year mattress warranty is no promise of durability. Mattress warranties are prorated like tire warranties and in a few years may reach the point where shipping costs outweigh—or nearly outweigh—the warranty's value. So, as a practical matter, the warranties protect mainly against mattress sets that are defective when they are relatively new.

Comfort. While firmness is important, conformity may be more important, especially to someone with a bad back. A properly conforming mattress should mold itself to the shape of your body. It should give a little under your shoulders and hips while still supporting the small of your back or waist. When your position changes, the mattress should spring back quickly and readjust itself to your new shape.

The only way to find a comfortable mattress is to lie down on several models. You may have to try out model after model to find out what level of firmness and conformity is right for you. Do a lot of sitting down, lying down, and rolling over on the mattresses you test. Try out your favorite sleeping position. If you share a mattress with someone, you should both do the testing.

In general, the more a sleeping surface allows air to circulate and body moisture to dissipate, the better. Vent openings help air exchange, but for most purposes a mattress breathes satisfactorily through the ticking and stitch holes.

The mattress set that's delivered to your home won't be the same one you saw in the showroom. Take a close look at the one that's delivered. Especially examine the fabric seams for unevenness. This could cause the bed to look curved or, worse, it may indicate a seam with insufficient depth—a sign that the seam may pull apart prematurely.

Take a look, too, at the inside of the box-spring foundation. You'll need to unstaple a bit of the thin dust shield on the bottom, but it's easily reattached. Look for wood that is split, cracked, warped, knotted, or otherwise obviously unequal to the task of providing a long, problem-free bed life.

Buy a foundation with corner guards, which help protect fabric from chafing against metal corners of the bed frame.

MICROWAVE CAKE BAKING

Cake mixes intended for baking in a microwave oven may be improved by making a few simple changes in the recipe. These changes can also work with conventional cake mixes that are baked in a microwave oven.

Here's what to do:

• Mix the batter with an electric mixer until it is completely smooth. This gives the cake a better "crumb," or texture.

• Line the bottom of the baking pan with a circle of waxed paper, and put another circle on top of the batter. This prevents a skin from forming on the cake.

• To bake the cake, set it in its pan on an inverted dinner plate in the oven. This helps bake the cake evenly.

• Begin by baking on a low wattage (power level), such as the Defrost setting, for 5 minutes with a light-colored cake; a couple of minutes longer with a chocolate cake. Then rotate the cake half a turn and bake it on High (full power) for $1\frac{1}{2}$

to 2 minutes. Finally, rotate the cake again and bake it another
1½ to 2 minutes—again on High.

MICROWAVE COOKWARE

Once you start using a microwave oven, you'll find yourself
changing old habits. One of them is what you cook in. You'll
make hot chocolate in the same cup you drink from. You'll
heat dinner right on your plate. And your stainless-steel cookware will be left hanging on the wall. Metal reflects microwave
energy—use a metal pot in a microwave oven and you'll get
either a cold meal or a damaged oven.

Many common kitchen items are fine for microwave cooking. Bacon cooks well on paper towels. You can defrost foods
right in their plastic freezer containers (with the cover off),
so long as you're careful not to heat the food enough to
melt the plastic. You can even heat food in straw serving
baskets.

Most ceramic or glass casseroles and baking dishes for use
in a regular oven also work in a microwave oven. Such utensils
cost a lot less than many dishes designed for microwave use.
An "old-fashioned" glass dish may suit your needs just fine.
Still, if you use a microwave a lot, you may want some cookware made specifically for the purpose.

A utensil's shape affects its performance in a microwave
oven. Round pans are superior for casseroles and meat loaf;
in rectangular ones, food in the corners tends to overcook.
Food also cooks more evenly when spread out in a shallow
pan. Most glass and ceramic microwave utensils can also be
used in a regular oven, if it's no hotter than 375°F to 400°F.
Few, if any, microwave pots and pans are usable on a range
top. Plastic microwave utensils may also be used in a regular
oven, but they may give off an unpleasant odor.

Clever design gives many microwave utensils versatility.
Casserole lids, for example, may be usable as cooking vessels.

Some open roasting racks double as baking trays. Others come with a trivet to use when roasting and remove when baking. A few racks come with a cover to help keep food from drying out and spattering during cooking.

Food browns better in a microwave oven when you use a special browning dish, but still not as appetizingly as when cooked the traditional way. Grilled cheese sandwiches turn out pale and unevenly cooked—the cheese melts before the bread shows much color. If you don't like microwaved roasts, you don't need a special roasting rack. Microwave ovens also don't bake well, so baking utensils aren't essential.

To see if one of your nonmetal dishes or utensils is usable in a microwave, set the oven on High and put the dish inside for about 8 minutes. If the dish stays fairly cool to the touch, it's probably all right for microwave use. But don't use good china or dishes with a decorative metal trim in a microwave. Be careful of pottery, which may have metal in the glaze or impurities in the clay.

MICROWAVE OVENS

A microwave oven can't substitute fully for a regular kitchen oven. Traditional ovens cook food from the outside in. Microwave cooking is more complex, and an ordinary microwave oven can't produce a roast turkey with crispy skin or a nicely browned roast beef.

Some microwave ovens have a browning element, and there are other models that combine the virtues of a regular oven with those of a microwave appliance (microwave-convection ovens). There's even a combination microwave-oven/toaster-oven/broiler.

But unless you are assembling a family of kitchen appliances from scratch, chances are you will find that the typical microwave oven's chief utility lies in its ability to do the things for which it was originally designed: heating, reheating, thawing, and cooking such things as baked potatoes, some varieties of fish, vegetables, and bacon.

Size. Microwave ovens are often classified by capacity:

Subcompact:	Interior 0.5 cubic foot (cu ft) or less
Compact:	Interior 0.6 to 0.7 cu ft
Midsize:	Interior 0.8 to 1 cu ft
Full-size:	Interior larger than 1 cu ft

Unfortunately, there's no really meaningful standardization from one maker to the next. And to add to the confusion there is no consistent relationship between an oven's exterior size and its cooking capacity. Not only do an oven's outer dimensions have to fit the space available in your kitchen, the oven's interior must be large enough to accommodate the cookware you will be using. You might want to take along a favorite casserole dish (one that's suitable for microwave cooking) when you shop to help you check an oven's interior space.

Speed. A magnetron is the part that generates a microwave oven's invisible high-energy cooking rays. In most full-size ovens, the magnetron produces about 700 watts of power for cooking. High power speeds up defrosting. You can also speed up the roasting of a turkey by cooking it partially in a microwave oven, then transferring the bird to a regular oven to finish up and crisp the skin.

A subcompact or compact microwave oven produces between 200 and 500 watts of power and is too small to hold a turkey. The average small oven takes about 30 percent longer than a full-size model to do the same job. This may mean only a minute, more or less, in added cooking time for a small item—one baked potato, for instance. But for a larger dish, such as a casserole, the difference would be 10 or 15 minutes.

Microwave cooking instructions tend to be approximations. You will probably find it necessary to adjust the recommended cooking times in recipes or on food packages.

Features. The controls on a deluxe microwave oven are quite complex, incorporating a great deal of automation. You still have the option of setting it by hand, bypassing the fancy controls. But this raises the question of whether you bought and paid for features you don't really need or want. In that case, give serious thought to buying a less deluxe unit.

Controls. Because exact timing is important in microwave cookery, electronic controls are a convenience. They let you set even the shortest cooking time exactly. Dial-type mechanical timers are less precise and are generally found on less expensive units. An electronic control's touch pad should be laid out logically, with numbers arranged more or less like those on a push-button telephone.

Power Levels. Five power-level settings are enough for any cooking task, even though a great many models offer ten or more.

Sensors and Probes. A sensor detects moisture escaping from covered food and is able to "figure" the necessary power level and cooking time automatically. Sensors are especially handy for cooking vegetables and reheating foods.

A probe functions similarly to a meat thermometer and is most useful for such bulky foods as casseroles.

Programming. Some microwave ovens come preprogrammed with a memory for cooking a variety of common foods. All you have to do is punch in the weight of the food (and the kind of food). The machine does the rest. You can also program instructions of your own for special dishes and then store them in the oven's memory.

Turntable. One peculiarity of microwave cooking is the existence of "dead" spots inside the oven where cooking proceeds at a snail's pace compared with what's happening at other spots within the same cooking space. This is the reason why you have to move food around during the course of cooking, despite many manufacturers' efforts to provide various devices for that purpose. Ovens with turntables that rotate as the food cooks don't necessarily make food cook more evenly; they do make the cooking process more predictable. On the negative side, a turntable reduces an oven's capacity, because the corners become unavailable. This can be especially limiting if the oven has a small capacity to begin with. If you intend using a microwave mainly for reheating food or for auxiliary cooking, you can get by without a turntable, perhaps adding a wind-up accessory turntable later on—if you find it necessary.

Safety. Microwave energy needs to be carefully confined to the inside of the oven. Once the oven turns off, there's no energy left over, and there's no residual energy in the food. But because of the potential for injury if there is any microwave leakage to the outside while the oven is on, the U.S. Bureau of Radiological Health has set standards for microwave oven leakage. A door seal on modern models minimizes microwave leakage even when slight gaps develop between the door and the oven. Furthermore, all ovens have at least two interlocks to prevent the oven from working if the door isn't tightly shut. Even so, it's probably a good idea to stay several feet away from the appliance when it is on, to minimize your exposure (this applies especially to children).

If you use the right kind of cooking utensil, it won't become hot in the course of cooking, except from the heat conducted to it from the hot food—but that can be hot enough. It's a good idea to use potholders when you remove food from the oven or when you shift the position of what's being cooked.

When you remove a lid or plastic wrap, be careful of escaping steam. And when you eat microwaved food, be cautious (and warn the family) about very hot spots in foods with fillings or mixed textures, such as fruit tarts and blueberry muffins.

Minerals *(see Vitamin Supplements)*

Moisturizers *(see Skin Moisturizers)*

MORTGAGE LOANS
Don't assume that when a lender accepts a mortgage application the interest rate is then fixed and will not increase before the loan closes.

In many cases, a mortgage lock-in is based on an oral agreement. Borrowers have no written assurance from the lender that the lower rate quoted when the loan was approved will still be in effect at the closing. Even with a written commitment, some lenders try to wriggle out of a lock-in through escape clauses in the fine print. Since most lock-ins are limited to a specific time period (usually 60 or 90 days), some lenders get out of the deal by dragging out the approval process.

Some states have taken action designed to force lenders to honor a mortgage commitment. A minimum disclosure should include:

- a statement of the maximum loan-processing time
- the interest rate and points
- a statement of whether or not the lender will "lock in" the terms

Try to obtain a loan agreement that requires a lender to honor a lock-in unless the delay is the borrower's fault.

MORTGAGE PAYMENTS
If you already have a mortgage or are in the market for a new one, you can probably save tens of thousands of dollars by "investing" in your mortgage. Take advantage of one of several new types of mortgage that have an *accelerated payment schedule*. By simply avoiding interest payments, you may net

more money than you would by earning interest on more liquid investments.

Rather than spending or investing cash elsewhere, consider plowing it back into savings in your house. After all, your home is one investment that has paid off handsomely in the past and will probably continue to do so in the future. With a little self-discipline you can probably squeeze out slightly more money each month to help prepay the existing mortgage.

To prepay, merely notify the lender that the extra amount should go directly for repayment of principal, not for interest. You may want to write a separate check to ensure that the lender services your loan properly. Keep track of how much extra principal you've paid, and compare your figures with the year-end statement issued by your mortgage holder.

Even taking into account the lost tax deductions and the lost income the extra payments might have earned in other investments, you are still likely to come out ahead by paying off your loan early.

MOVING

If you move, one thing you can expect is a big bill. Not very long ago, the average household move (transporting some 6,000 pounds about 1,100 miles) cost more than $2,500.

Most moving vans haul the belongings of more than one customer. To determine the weight of your things, the mover weighs the truck, with whatever load is already on it, on a certified scale, then loads your things and weighs the truck again. What you pay depends on the difference between the initial weight (called the tare) and the weight after loading (called the gross).

Estimates. You can often save money by getting at least three estimates. There are three types of estimate—binding, nonbinding, and a hybrid of the two.

With a binding estimate, the estimated cost is final; the mover won't even weigh your things on moving day. A binding estimate is generally the best kind, even though it may be slightly higher than a nonbinding one. A nonbinding estimate is desirable only if, at the time of the estimate, you're still unsure about what you'll be moving. Many movers also offer an estimate that binds them but not you. Under that arrangement, the mover issues a binding estimate but weighs your things on moving day anyway. If the actual weight of your shipment is more than estimated, you pay only the estimated rate. If the weight is less than estimated, you pay only for the actual weight.

Once you decide on a company, the mover you choose will draw up an *order for service*. This isn't a contract. If you delay your move or decide not to use the company, you can cancel without penalty. You'll sign the actual contract, called the *bill of lading*, on packing day (or moving day, if you're doing the packing yourself).

Don't sign an order for service or a bill of lading unless it mentions specific dates for pickup and delivery. If a mover fails to pick up or deliver your shipment on time, you may be able to collect for out-of-pocket expenses during the delay by filing an inconvenience or delay claim with your mover.

Damage. Before moving, review your homeowners insurance policy to see whether your possesions will be covered for damage, breakage, or loss during the move. If your move isn't covered, you can usually obtain coverage either from your insurance company or from the mover.

If anything is lost or damaged during the move, get a claim form from your agent or from the mover's home office. The sooner you file, the sooner you have a chance to collect. But in any case, your claim must be filed within 9 months.

If you can't resolve a dispute through the regular claims process, you can take the moving company to court or request that your case go to arbitration. You can request arbitration by writing the American Movers Conference, Dispute Settlement Program, 440 Army-Navy Drive, Arlington, VA 22202. Your letter must be sent within 60 days after the final offer or denial on your claim has been made in writing by the mover. The decision is supposed to be made within 60 days after receipt of all necessary forms.

MUTUAL FUNDS

A welter of mutual funds compete for your investment dollars. How can you identify good performers?

The Standard and Poor's index of 500 stocks is a useful yardstick. A fund worthy of your money should outperform the S&P in most years. A fund salesperson should be able to show you, in writing, how a particular fund has done compared with the S&P 500. You might also want to send for recent prospectuses and compare funds on your own.

Here are six types of stock mutual funds:

• *Balanced funds* invest in a fairly even mixture of stocks and bonds.

• *Income funds* invest in a flexible mixture of bonds and stocks that pay high dividends.

• *Long-term growth funds* (also called *growth funds*) invest in stocks of companies with rising earnings. The primary objective of a growth fund is capital gains (appreciation in the price of the stocks, as opposed to dividends).

• *Growth-and-income funds* aim for a balance between dividends and capital gains.

• *Maximum-capital-gains funds* (also called *aggressive growth funds*) try for the highest possible capital gains. They differ from growth funds by investing in the shares of smaller companies, or by using borrowed money in an attempt to magnify investment results, or both.

- *Specialized funds* invest in a narrowly defined sector, such as gold and gold mining.

The following two types of funds are not stock funds:

- *Money-market funds* invest in large bank certificates of deposit and short-term IOUs issued by corporations and government agencies. The risk is negligible. While solid yields are virtually assured, spectacular gains, like those sometimes achieved with stock funds, are essentially precluded.
- *Bond funds* involve more risk than money-market funds, because bonds can rise and fall in value. In general, the potential gains or losses from a bond fund are smaller than those from a stock fund.

OILS AND FATS FOR COOKING (*see also* FISH AND HEALTH)

Oil is simply fat that's liquid at room temperature. Oil and fat are the most concentrated sources of energy in the human diet. They also carry vitamins A, D, E, and K, and they're the chief source of essential fatty acids, which the body can't manufacture on its own.

But fat that isn't expended as body heat and energy is easily converted to body fat. So a high-fat diet can lead to obesity and all its complications. Furthermore, consumption of certain types of fat, termed *saturated*, can contribute to elevated blood cholesterol levels, a high-risk factor in heart attacks. It makes sense, then, to cut some fat from your diet—especially the saturated kind.

For nearly 40 years there has been a broad dietary shift toward fat and oil from vegetable sources, because they contain fewer saturated and more *polyunsaturated* fats than animal fats do. There's been a parallel shift toward liquid oil, which is usually less saturated than solid fat.

While saturated fat in the diet tends to increase the blood's cholesterol level, polyunsaturated fat tends to lower that level. *Mono-unsaturated* fat (the kind found in olive oil) may have a similar effect. Accordingly, people with elevated cholesterol readings are often advised, among other things, to reduce their intake of saturated fat and increase their intake of polyunsaturated fat.

Vegetable Oils. Except for coconut and palm oil, common ingredients in a host of supermarket foods (particularly crackers and cookies), vegetable oil is relatively low in saturated fat. But there are some differences among them. Canola oil is the least saturated (about 6 percent) of currently available vegetable oils. Safflower and sunflower oils are slightly more saturated (about 10 percent). Soy and corn oils are a little more so (about 14 percent). Peanut oil is the most saturated (about 20 percent). To put these numbers in perspective: butterfat is about 60 percent saturated.

Most vegetable oil is naturally high in polyunsaturates (about 50 to 80 percent). Olive oil and canola oil, however, present quite a different profile. They are composed mainly of mono-unsaturated fat, which means they are not high in saturated fat, nor in polyunsaturates either.

Shortening made from vegetable oil has a higher saturated-fat content than the oils from which it is made. This is because it's been changed from liquid to solid by *hydrogenation,* a process in which exposure to hydrogen saturates oil to some extent. (Hydrogenation has another function: it helps retard spoilage. Even certain liquid oils, such as soybean oil, are routinely hydrogenated somewhat to keep them fresh longer.) All-vegetable-oil shortening has a saturation of between 25 and 30 percent.

Shortening that contains meat fat is even more saturated— above 40 percent. Meat fat also contains cholesterol in significant amounts, while vegetable fats and oils contain none.

A Tip on Deep Frying. Many people discard cooking oil after each session of deep frying. High-quality oil should remain fit for more frying if it's filtered through cheesecloth or a fine sieve to remove burned food particles that might speed its deterioration. Since the used oil has undoubtedly suffered some degradation anyway, infuse it, by one-quarter to one-third, with fresh oil at each new use. This infusion will raise the smoke point again, thereby keeping to a minimum the tendency of an oil to begin smoking at an ever lower temperature as it decomposes with use.

ORANGE JUICE

A morning glass of orange juice is a good way to meet your daily requirement of vitamin C. A 6-ounce serving of juice from frozen concentrate just about provides an adult's U.S. Recommended Daily Allowance (U.S. RDA) of 60 milligrams of vitamin C.

Orange juice is also a good source of potassium, as are many other common foods, such as meat, potatoes, bananas, and peanut butter. Since potassium is so abundant, healthy people rarely, if ever, develop a potassium deficiency. (Indeed, there is no Recommended Daily Allowance for potassium. Typical daily intakes range from 800 to 5,000 milligrams.) People who take potassium-depleting medication (some drugs used for treating hypertension, for example) may need extra potassium. This is something to discuss with your doctor.

While orange juice is a nutritious drink, it's not a diet drink. Ounce for ounce, orange juice has about as many calories as cola or beer: roughly 80 calories per 6-ounce serving. More than 10 percent of orange juice is fruit sugar. That's why people on a diet are advised to *eat* an orange rather than drink a glassful of juice, the equivalent of three or four oranges.

Orange juice packaged in a box (not to be confused with chilled juice in the dairy case) is heated, quickly cooled, then packed in multilayer laminated cartons without any air space. The "aseptic" description of this packaging refers to the closed, germ-free environment in which the packing takes place. Like cans, aseptic cartons can be stored at room temperature and packed in a lunchbox or bought from a vending machine without fear of spoilage.

While boxed juice may be easy to store, its taste is just about on a par with canned juice, and is prone to have the same metallic off-flavor. Consider it only for situations in which the package's convenience and portability demand that you put up with poor flavor.

Besides freshly squeezed juice, the best-tasting orange juices are frozen concentrates and chilled juices. Of the two, the frozen variety tastes better and often costs less. If you think you are buying a higher-quality product when you buy chilled juice, try switching to frozen concentrate and stop carrying home the extra water. This assumes, of course, that your tap water tastes good enough not to affect the taste of reconstituted frozen juice.

If frozen and chilled juices aren't stored properly, their flavor—and their vitamin C content—can deteriorate. Use an airtight jar, because both the orange flavor and vitamin C degrade rapidly in the presence of air.

If you like the convenience of chilled juice, consider buying it by the quart, rather than in the 2-quart size. This will help to preserve freshness.

OVEN CLEANERS

Most oven cleaners contain sodium hydroxide, or lye, one of the most dangerous substances sold for household use. This is because baked-on oven dirt is too tough for ordinary cleaners. Lye causes a chemical reaction, decomposing the stuck-on fats and sugars into soapy compounds you can wash away. Lye-containing oven cleaners are also corrosively alkaline.

Before using a cleaner containing lye, protect yourself with a long-sleeved shirt and rubber gloves. If you use an aerosol, wear a paper dust mask and goggles. Cover nearby floors, counters, and other surfaces with newspaper.

Packaging affects the convenience and safety of oven clean-ers. *Pads* don't create airborne particles of lye and are handy for quick spot-cleaning. *Aerosols* are easy to apply but are apt to get on gaskets, heating elements, and sometimes on your face. A broad, concave button on the aerosol can makes it harder to misdirect the spray than a small button. An *adjustable pump spray* can be a real annoyance. The adjustable nozzle produces anything from a stream to a misty, broad spray. The stream doesn't cover much and splatters, and the spray is diffuse and too easy to inhale. *Brush-on jelly* is tedious to use and almost impossible to keep from spattering.

There is a brighter side, however. You *can* buy at least one brand of oven cleaner that is made without lye and that is not hazardous. This type of cleaner won't be quite as effective as some lye cleaners, but a second application should do a fin-ishing job to please even the most demanding homemaker.

Even if you don't have a self-cleaning oven or one with a continuous-clean finish (on which, incidentally, you can't use an oven cleaner), you shouldn't feel sentenced forever to the hard labor of oven cleaning. An oven in continual use can reach a steady state at which grime burns off at the same rate it accumulates. Serious spills, such as when a cake overflows its pan, can be scraped up after the oven cools. A little dirt in the oven never hurt anybody. A little oven cleaner might.

PAIN RELIEVERS

There are only three pain relievers available without a doctor's prescription—aspirin, acetaminophen, and ibuprofen. For the vast majority of people, occasional use of any of these three analgesics is quite safe. But each of them can cause unpleasant or serious side effects in certain individuals.

Aspirin has remained popular because it works. Two 325-milligram (5-grain) tablets at 4-hour intervals will relieve mild-to-moderate pain and reduce fever. Aspirin's action against inflammation also makes it an important drug in treating arthritis. And it acts to inhibit the blood from clotting, a characteristic that has led to its use by people who have had heart-attack or stroke warnings.

Aspirin can irritate the stomach, however. Heavy users, such as people with arthritis, face an increased risk of serious stomach bleeding from ulceration and inflammation.

Don't count on *buffered* aspirin being faster-acting or more soothing to the stomach than plain aspirin, although enteric-coated aspirin does cause less stomach irritation. These tablets have a special coating that prevents them from dissolving until they reach the small intestine.

A small percentage of individuals are aspirin-sensitive—often those with severe asthma or chronic hives—and must avoid aspirin altogether. Anyone with ulcers or other stomach problems should avoid taking aspirin, except under a physician's supervision. Pregnant women should also forgo aspirin, especially during the last 3 months of pregnancy.

Children with flu or chicken pox should *never* be given aspirin. Studies indicate that aspirin given to children with these illnesses may cause *Reye's syndrome*, a rare but often fatal disorder.

Acetaminophen shares aspirin's ability to reduce fever and relieve mild-to-moderate pain. But it lacks aspirin's anti-inflammatory effect. Acetaminophen's main advantage is that it's gentler to the stomach than aspirin. While acetaminophen causes few side effects of any kind in normal doses, in larger doses it's not totally nonirritating to the stomach.

One group of people should avoid acetaminophen: those who drink a lot of alcohol risk liver damage, even with moderate doses of the drug.

Ibuprofen is the first new nonprescription analgesic in nearly 35 years. Ibuprofen and aspirin seem to work the same way in the body. Both drugs inhibit the production of prostaglandins, hormonelike chemicals involved in causing pain and inflammation. Although both drugs increase the chances of stomach upset, ibuprofen isn't considered quite as irritating as aspirin. But it is more irritating than acetaminophen.

In general, anyone who should avoid aspirin for any reason should also avoid ibuprofen—and vice versa. Both drugs work the same way and can cause similar side effects. When ibuprofen was approved for over-the-counter sale a few years ago, some physicians pointed out that nonprescription ibuprofen could pose serious health risks of possible kidney damage for certain people. The most recent FDA conclusion, however, is that "it does not appear that over-the-counter ibuprofen has caused either frequent or serious effects" of any kind. The FDA spokesperson did say, however, that the FDA had reports of 14 cases of kidney problems among people who were taking over-the-counter ibuprofen.

Milligram for milligram, aspirin and acetaminophen are

equally potent for relieving pain—two regular-strength tablets—650 milligrams (10 grains)—can take care of most headaches and other minor aches and pains. Ibuprofen appears to offer some pain-relief advantages over aspirin and acetaminophen. Studies suggest that one 200-milligram tablet provides slightly better pain relief than 650 milligrams of either aspirin or acetaminophen. Ibuprofen is especially helpful for treating pain from "soft tissue" injuries such as strains and sprains. It has also done well in studies involving pain relief after dental surgery. But ibuprofen's main advantage is its effectiveness against menstrual pain.

Ringing in the Ears. Some doctors advise patients suffering from ringing in the ears (tinnitus) to avoid taking aspirin because it might aggravate the problem. In addition to being a symptom in numerous ear disorders, tinnitus is also a side effect of high-dose aspirin therapy.

Ibuprofen usually does not produce this side effect. But a small percentage of ibuprofen users *do* experience tinnitus, roughly 1 to 3 percent of those taking more than 1,200 milligrams of ibuprofen daily.

PAINTING A CONCRETE FLOOR

Painting concrete isn't as easy as painting the walls in a room, primarily because concrete can be a finicky material. If you want to do a good job, make sure the floor is clean, dry, dust- and grease-free, and properly primed. Don't treat concrete with muriatic acid before painting. Despite the benefits, such treatment is too hazardous an undertaking.

You have to match the type of paint to the kind of use and abuse the floor will sustain. A garage area or an outdoor surface such as a poolside patio probably needs a tougher paint coating than a basement family room. If you're planning to paint outdoor steps or a walkway, you'll want a durable paint that isn't very slippery when wet. Your choice will be easier if the floor is sound and will rarely be exposed to water.

The toughest finish you can put on a concrete floor is a two-package epoxy. (You may find epoxy labeled as an ingredient of some paints, but unless the paint is the two-package kind, it probably won't work very well.) Epoxy paint, however, is quite slippery when wet with water. If you don't require such a glossy finish, a latex paint is your best choice. Latex paint goes on easily and dries quickly. Its resistance to water is good and it's not slippery when wet.

Paints *(see House Paints and Stains; Latex Interior Paints; Painting a Concrete Floor)*

PANCAKE MIXES
The best pancakes come from a favorite do-it-yourself recipe or, failing that, from prepared mixes that require you to add fresh eggs, oil, and milk. You sacrifice some taste but save some time if you use a complete mix that requires only water or milk to complete the batter.

Dry mixes are the cheapest to use, usually costing less than a nickel per pancake. Pancakes made with frozen batter cost about a dime apiece, while frozen ready-made products cost as much as 18 cents each. Frozen batters also require advance planning because they take at least a day to thaw. You can't defrost them quickly in a microwave oven; doing so will cook the batter.

Pancakes Made from Scratch. Here's a recipe developed by Consumers Union for what might be called the Almost Perfect Pancake. The ingredients cost about as much as a good prepared mix, and the pancakes take about the same time to make as with an add-everything mix.

Almost Perfect Pancakes

    2   cups white all-purpose flour
    2   tbsp baking powder

¼ cup sugar
2 large eggs
2 tbsp oil
2 cups whole milk

1. Let the griddle preheat while you prepare the batter. (If the griddle has a thermostat, set it for 400°F; otherwise, set the control for Medium High.) Grease the griddle very lightly with vegetable oil, margarine, or butter.
2. Sift the dry ingredients together in a large bowl. In a separate bowl, beat the eggs, oil, and milk until well blended. Add the liquids to the dry ingredients, stirring lightly with a wire whisk or a fork until the batter is creamy with some small lumps.
3. Spoon or ladle the batter onto the hot griddle. Turn the pancakes when their edges look dry and bubbles cover the top. Flip them only once; more often will give them a tough texture.

The recipe yields about 19 4-inch pancakes.

For less dense pancakes, separate the eggs when you mix the batter. Add the yolks with the other liquids; whip the whites until soft peaks form and add them after you've combined the other ingredients.

For thinner pancakes, add more milk or water to the batter.

PANCAKE SYRUP
Real maple syrup tastes best. It costs 3 to 4 times as much per ounce as products containing just a little maple syrup, or none at all. But because genuine maple syrup is extremely sweet, you'll probably use it more sparingly than the synthetic variety. Pure maple syrup is by far the best choice if you are watching your sodium intake.

PANTY HOSE

Nylon is just about the perfect material for hose. It's strong, resilient, resistant to abrasion, capable of being spun very fine and smooth, and is unaffected by perspiration. But manufacturing methods that emphasize one of those qualities often do so at the expense of others. So, until fairly recently, you couldn't find stockings that were simultaneously sheer, silky, stretchy, and strong.

Sheerness, support, and *control* don't have any standardized definitions, so those words on a hosiery package are often more advertisement than description. *Sheer,* for example, may mean the hose are sheerer than some other hose sold by the same company. Or it may mean the hose are sheerer than, say, a pair of cotton socks. Or *sheer* might carry the same meaning as it does in *sheer pleasure.* The word is often a part of the brand name.

Sheerness is often at odds with stretch as well as with strength. Both the elasticity and strength of nylon can be increased by adding even a small amount of a synthetic fiber called spandex. Stockings with spandex hold the leg in, supporting it and helping to keep ankles and feet from swelling. But until recent years, spandex made *support hose* bulky and thick—the hose of choice mainly for women who must be on their feet for long periods.

More than 10 years ago, manufacturers discovered how to spin spandex into finer strands and how to wrap the strands with nylon, a technique that makes the fiber silkier yet tougher than plain spandex. The result is the so-called *light-support hose,* which are popular as much for their comfort as for the support they provide. Encouraged, manufacturers knit even finer spandex threads into very sheer hose. Hose that really offer support will usually say so somewhere on the label.

Adding spandex to the panty part of panty hose has produced yet another category of hose, *control-top hose.* This variety isn't girdlelike, however—the spandex serves more to smooth things over than hold it all in.

Features. There are several things to look for in panty hose:

• The color of the panty is the only difference you're likely to find between regular hose and products that advertise themselves as combination underpants/panty hose.

• A wide, reinforced waistband helps hold up sheer-to-the-waist hose and doesn't bind the way a narrow band does.

• A crotch panel usually makes hose fit more comfortably, especially in queen size. A panel made of cotton breathes better than one made of nylon—which is important whether or not you wear underpants.

• A hole in the toe can be a big nuisance. Buy hose with reinforced toes.

• Very sheer hose can be durable if they contain a bit of spandex.

• Washing panty hose loose in the washing machine shortens their life. Panty hose last longer if you wash them by hand or use a net bag in the washer.

Price. You can generally get the best prices by buying your hose through the mail. The real bargains are the imperfects, also sold only through the mail. Companies say the flaws in these hose are cosmetic—a few strands less per square inch, a panty that's not quite the right hue, and so on. This is likely to be true. In most cases, you won't be able to find the imperfection. The companies also claim that the flaws won't affect wear. This is also likely to be true.

PAPER TOWELS

The strongest, most absorbent towels tend to be among the premium-priced brands. But that doesn't make these towels the best value. For simple spills or small mop-ups, you may want to keep a roll of cheap paper towels handy.

If you really want to get the best price, you'll have to take a pocket calculator to the supermarket. You'll then be able to compute the price per square foot (or per 100 square feet). It's true that towels are perforated and that the price per square foot is affected in a practical way by how much towel you have to tear off the roll each time you use one. Nevertheless, the careful shopper may find some satisfaction in trying to "beat the game," at least once in a while.

A cents-off coupon or a special store sale may make an otherwise expensive brand a good buy. But towels in two-roll or three-roll packs don't necessarily give you a price break; a multiple-roll pack may be no cheaper per 100 towels or per 100 square feet than single rolls of the same brand.

PEANUT BUTTER
With or without jelly, a peanut butter sandwich is a good lunch for a child or an adult. It provides a nice balance of protein, carbohydrates, and calories. The table on the next page shows how peanut butter stacks up against other common sandwich fillings. (Our peanut butter sandwich uses 3 tablespoons of peanut butter as a serving, not the skimpy 2 tablespoons most jars list on their labels.)

Protein. A peanut is not a nut but a legume, in the same family as the pea and the bean. This explains its high protein content. A peanut butter sandwich provides about one-fourth of the daily protein requirement for an adult, more for a child.

The protein in peanut butter is also a bargain. The 3-tablespoon sandwich, with jelly added, costs about 28 cents. It provides 16 grams of protein at a cost of about $8 per pound of protein. A cheese sandwich's protein would cost something like $11.50 per pound; bologna's, $16.50; tuna's, $9.50.

COMPARING SANDWICHES

	Peanut butter, 3 tbsp*	Cheese food, 2 oz (with mayo)	Bologna, 2 oz (with mayo)	Chunk light tuna, 2 oz (with mayo)
Protein	24% of U.S. RDA	24% of U.S. RDA	17% of U.S. RDA	29% of U.S. RDA
Vitamin A	—	11	1	1
Thiamin	19	16	16	15
Riboflavin	11	24	13	11
Niacin	40	9	16	40
Vitamin B_6	10	1	6	11
Vitamin B_{12}	—	11	13	40
Vitamin C	—	—	16	—
Calcium	8	39	7	7
Iron	14	11	13	11
Zinc	10	14	8	5
Sodium (mg)	476	998	891	553
Calories	410	413	405	290
Fat (gm)	26	27	29	13
Carbohydrates (gm)	33	28	25	24
Cost (cents)	24.6	38.7	39.2	39.5

Note: Figures based on U.S. Recommended Daily Allowances, which should meet daily dietary needs of adults and children over 4. Sandwiches on white bread; mayonnaise used was 1 tbsp.
*Tbsp grape jelly adds 55 calories and about 3 cents to cost.

Fat. Peanut butter is also a relatively fatty food (unlike other legumes, the peanut itself is nearly half fat), with about 355 calories per 3-tablespoon serving. But little of that fat is saturated. The ratio of saturated fat to total fat for peanut butter is only about 20 percent, compared with about 65 percent for American cheese and 40 percent for bologna. There's no significant difference in total fat or saturated-fat content between the brands that contain added hydrogenated oil and the "natural" brands. (Natural peanut butter is made only of ground-up peanuts, sometimes with salt.)

Sugar and Sodium. The differences are greater in the sugar and salt content. Products that have added sweeteners may contain plain sugar, dextrose, corn syrup, or molasses. Natural peanut butter contains only 5 to 9 percent sugar, the level that occurs naturally in peanuts.

Products without added salt contain virtually no sodium— 15 or fewer milligrams per serving. But even peanut butters with added salt have fairly low sodium levels (about 180 to 250 milligrams) when compared with foods such as cheese and bologna.

Storage. Refrigeration extends the shelf life of peanut butter, especially in the summer. But peanut butter should keep all right at room temperature for several weeks.

Because refrigeration helps keep the oil from separating, natural peanut butter should be mixed right after purchase and then refrigerated. Mixing natural peanut butter isn't very easy; it requires patience and a slow stirring with a sturdy knife.

PERSONAL SECURITY

A few simple steps can help protect you from street crime. The National Crime Prevention Council (NCPC) recommends that men carry their wallet in a front pants pocket to thwart pickpockets, rather than in a back pocket or front jacket pocket. Men may want to consider wearing a money belt, since few muggers think of asking victims to remove their belts— except in places where the belts are common, such as Las Vegas.

Choose a wallet with a fabric exterior, which is tougher to remove from a pocket than a slick leather one. Finally, keep your cash and credit cards separate.

The NCPC advises women to carry a wallet with important

identification and credit cards in a pocket separate from their handbag, and to use a handbag with a long strap worn across the body.

Pill Removers *(see Fabric Pill Removers)*

PIZZA: FROZEN
Pizza, one of America's favorite foods, doesn't fare so well when frozen. Each of the ingredients in a typical pizza tends to suffer under extreme temperatures:

Cheese. Mozzarella, the basic pizza cheese, is normally bought fresh and must be consumed quickly. It doesn't keep or freeze well—the distinctive flavor shifts toward a cruder "cheesiness" when frozen, while the soft, stringy texture deteriorates into a drier, crumblier sort of ropiness. To counteract this tendency, most makers of frozen pizza use a low-moisture, part-skim-milk mozzarella cheese in their products.

Frozen sausage-and-pepperoni pizzas tend to stray even further—the mozzarella cheese in these products contains a low-moisture, part-skim-milk mozzarella cheese *substitute*. The substitute is made from casein (a constituent of milk), soybean oil, and a lot of additives.

This is why it's so difficult to detect more than a slight taste of mozzarella in frozen pizza. It's especially hard to pick up the flavors of Romano, Parmesan, or provolone cheeses even if the product lists them as ingredients.

Tomato Sauce. Sauces, too, suffer in freezing—their subtle blend of distinct flavors becomes blurred, as do the traditional sauce spices, oregano and basil. Olive oil in the sauce suffers the same fate.

Crust. The crust on frozen pizza doesn't quite match a crust made from a fresh yeast dough. The frozen crust is somewhat crackerlike or biscuitlike. It becomes crispy nearly all the way through, however, when you cook it. Some commercial pizza makers partially cook the crust before adding the toppings and freezing, apparently trying for a more uniformly crispy/chewy character in the finished product.

Nutrition. As a snack or as part of a quick meal, pizza fits nicely into a well-balanced diet. It's not low-calorie food, of course, but it does contribute very respectably to nutrition. For instance, pizza supplies a fair amount of vitamins A and C as well as iron, and the crust is a rather good source of the B vitamins.

Pizza is also a good source of protein. On average, a slice of meat-topped pizza contains about 20 grams, more than one-third of most people's Recommended Dietary Allowance (RDA) as set by the National Academy of Sciences/National Research Council. Cheese pizza also contains a lot of calcium, averaging about 422 milligrams a slice.

On average, expect about 450 calories from a serving of frozen pizza, regardless of its type.

Sodium-aware people should take note that a slice of frozen pizza contains around 1,000 milligrams of sodium, perhaps because the cheese and meat components are salty to begin with.

Plastic Bags (*see Garbage Bags*)

Portable Stereo Players (*see Walkabout Stereo Players*)

Pots and Pans (*see Cookware; Microwave Cookware*)

Power Lawn Mowers (*see Lawn Mowers*)

RACK STEREO SYSTEMS

A rack system—a sort of movable closet stacked with components from a single manufacturer, plus a pair of loudspeakers—makes it easy and convenient to buy stereo equipment. The components are supposedly matched to each other in capabilities and quality. You have to rely on the manufacturer's choices rather than on your own intuition or a clerk's recommendations.

But the biggest attraction of rack systems is also their biggest drawback: one or another of the components may be inferior. You won't know until you assemble the rack and try the components out. Although you can substitute components in some rack systems, doing so defeats the purpose of buying the system in the first place.

Buy a rack system only if you are in the market for an entire new stereo outfit, rather than want to upgrade your existing system. If you are satisfied with your present components but want to add a compact-disc (CD) player or replace the loudspeakers, it's best to shop around for each individual component.

RADON

Up to 20,000 Americans, it's estimated, will die this year from exposure to radon, a colorless, odorless gas. Formed from uranium, the gas is present almost everywhere and can easily seep into houses. Inhaling it or its decay products introduces radioactivity directly into the body. Only cigarette smoking is a surer road to lung cancer.

Happily, radon problems are easy to detect and, usually, to solve. Cheap ($10) activated-charcoal detectors can take radon readings in your basement in 3 to 7 days. Mail the detector to a lab and you should have results in a week or two. Your state radiological-health agency can give you the address of a qualified laboratory.

Radon is measured in picocuries per liter of air. (A picocurie is a trillionth of a curie, a unit of radiation.) If your lab results are 5 picocuries or less, your risk is fairly low. Readings of 20 picocuries and up, however, indicate need for action.

Between 5 and 20 picocuries, correction is called for, and it's wise to do a follow-up test. An alpha-track detector ($25 to $50) can be exposed in your family's living space for several months, then mailed to a lab. The results give a direct measure of your long-term average radon exposure.

Correcting a radon problem can be as simple as opening windows in your basement, installing a fan in the area, or caulking off the entry points of the gas. Heavy contamination may call for elaborate venting systems costing as much as $2,000 to install. For a fuller discussion of your options, consult the U.S. Environmental Protection Agency's (EPA's) booklet *Radon Reduction Methods: A Homeowner's Guide,* OPA-86-005. It's available through state radiological-health programs.

For even more detail, consult EPA's *Radon Reduction Techniques for Detached Houses, Technical Guidance,* EPA/625/5-86/019. Aimed at contractors, the publication is available from the Center for Environmental Research Information, Distribution, 26 W. St. Clair, Cincinnati, OH 45268. A thorough discussion of radon's risks, along with medical background and solutions, can be found in *Radon: A Homeowner's Guide to Detection and Control*. This book is available in bookstores or by mail for $10 plus $3 postage from Consumer Reports Books, 540 Barnum Ave., Bridgeport, CT 06608.

RANGES

Microwave ovens now do some of the tasks regular ovens once did. But when it comes to baking and broiling, you are still apt to rely on your range's oven. Today, most people buy a 30-inch-wide freestanding range.

Many people prefer cooktops with gas burners. Gas allows more precise control over heat, because there is no residual heat when you turn it off, as there is with electric elements. It is also good for those quick bursts of high heat necessary in wok cookery. Ranges with knobs that turn a half-circle or more allow finer adjustments than those that rotate only 90°.

Oven Cleaning. A *self-cleaning* oven incinerates food soil by attaining a temperature of a least 800°F and maintaining that temperature for a couple of hours (with the oven door automatically locked). All that's left after the oven cools down is an ashy residue, which wipes away easily.

A *continuous-cleaning* oven has a special, porous coating that supposedly spreads out spills and grease spatters. The object is to burn off dirt as it accumulates. In our experience, this kind of oven is no better and sometimes is worse than a plain oven with a shiny, conventional enamel surface. At least in a conventional oven you can clean the enamel when it gets too soiled to be tolerable. You *can't* clean a continuous-cleaning oven by hand: the surface won't tolerate it.

Self-cleaning ovens are much more commonly found in electric ranges than in gas models. In fact, more than half of all gas ranges sold have an oven that must be cleaned the old-fashioned way—the balance are either continuous-cleaning or self-cleaning.

A *built-in oven vent* carries away vapors during cooking and self-cleaning. The vent creates an additional cleaning chore by soiling either the backguard or the cooktop, depending on which way the vent faces. In some ranges the vent is not guarded, a problem because it becomes easy to drop something into the vent accidentally. Retrieving the dropped object could require a major disassembly of the oven.

Cooktop Cleaning. Since cooktops have to be cleaned by hand, some built-in features and design details can make the job easier. Look for:

- removable drip pans.
- controls on the vertical rather than the horizontal, so they don't get dirty quite so fast.
- seamless curves at corners and where the backguard meets the cooktop.
- a hinged cooktop that permits easy access to the space under the top burners or heating elements.
- plain trim. Avoid chrome side trim. Chrome may look good, but only when it's brand-new. Not only does chrome take continual wiping to remain shiny and spotless, it catches grease and dirt.
- porcelain-finished drip bowls under heating elements and burners. Shiny metal bowls may lose their shine soon after cooking begins. When cleaned, they may show scratches, and some may even rust after a time.

Reliability. In general, a gas range is less reliable in the long run than an electric. Gas ranges are more complicated than electrics because of a need for extra safety provisions and special control systems. Self-cleaning ranges of either type are less reliable than models cleaned manually.

Recording Tapes *(see Videotapes)*

Record-keeping *(see Household Record-keeping)*

REFRIGERATOR/FREEZERS
When you're buying a refrigerator, what do you look for? The basic choice for most people is a side-by-side or a top-freezer model.

A side-by-side model has some advantages. When open, its doors need about a foot less clearance in front than a top-freezer model does. Those inches can make a difference in a crowded kitchen. You also can store quick-turnover items in the middle of each compartment so you can get to them without stretching or stooping. And the tall, thin shape of each compartment makes it easy to find a stray jar of mayonnaise or an elusive package of frozen vegetables. With a top freezer, nothing in the refrigerator can be stored at eye level.

But a side-by-side refrigerator/freezer isn't for everyone. One reason is the higher initial price; another is that a side-by-side will use slightly more electricity than a top-freezer unit, even after adjusting for differences in capacity. And side-by-side refrigerator/freezers have a tendency to need more repairs more often than top freezers.

Convenience. There are a number of convenience features to consider:

Main Shelves. Except for a fixed shelf that covers one or both crispers, shelves in the main refrigerator compartment should be adjustable. A side-by-side model has at least four full-width shelves. Many top-freezer units have half-width shelves that provide extra flexibility—but also more chances to knock things over unless the shelves are aligned.

The main shelving in the freezer is usually plastic or wire—fixed in most side-by-sides, adjustable in most top freezers.

Side-by-side models have a utility bin or basket under the bottom shelf.

Door. Some side-by-sides have three doors, rather than the standard two. The third door conceals the ice maker and one small shelf. This allows you to get ice without opening the main freezer door and helps maintain freezer temperature at a steady level. Some models may have a juice-can dispenser built into the freezer door, which is a minor convenience at best. An ice maker, although handy for most households, takes up a lot of freezer space. On any model, detents to hold the door open are a good thing to have, as is a stop to keep the door from hitting an adjacent cabinet or appliance and becoming marred or even dented.

Door Shelves. Adjustable shelves are handy. Extra-deep shelves are good for holding six-packs or gallon milk containers. Some shelves are like bins—you can use them to tote their contents to a kitchen counter. Retainers should keep a door shelf's contents from toppling out when you open the door quickly. There should be at least one door compartment for butter or margarine. Its door should stay up when raised so you can get at the compartment's contents using one hand.

Special Shelves. Some models offer special-purpose shelving: racks to hold wine bottles or dispense beverage cans; a carousel; and the like.

Handles. Before you buy, try the doors to see if the handles are comfortable. There should be adequate space between the appliance's surface and the door handle to allow plenty of clearance for your knuckles, particularly if you wear a ring.

Cleaning. A refrigerator's condenser coil, which gets rid of the heat from inside the cabinet (and so makes it cold), may need to be cleaned every 3 months or so. The coil is often mounted just below the cabinet and tends to collect dust. Cleaning the coil is easier if you use a condenser-coil cleaning brush and a vacuum cleaner's crevice tool.

Bottom-mounted coils are usually the easiest to clean. Back-mounted coils don't collect as much dust, but you do have to move the refrigerator occasionally to deal with them.

Routine maintenance should include removing and cleaning the drip pan under the refrigerator. This pan, just behind the kickplate, collects water (and odors) during the automatic defrost cycle.

It is easiest to clean the inside of a refrigerator that has a seamless liner, generally made of plastic. A few liners are made of enameled or porcelainized steel or painted aluminum. Don't allow spills to drip into the freezer vents of any model: this can leave a lasting odor.

Temperature. The best average temperature for a refrigerator is 37°F. The freezer should be able to hold to 0°F, not only for long-term storage but also as extra protection against temperature fluctuations from defrosting and the like. Since freezers warm by 3° or 4° during the defrost cycle, and by 4° or 5° during ice making, an overwarm freezer can radically shorten the storage life of frozen foods. Use a refrigerator/freezer thermometer to monitor temperature and to make seasonal thermostat adjustments.

RUNNING SHOES

When it's time to shop for new running shoes, take the old ones with you. A knowledgeable shoe salesperson should check the old shoe soles for wear patterns. He or she should also ask pertinent questions about your running habits and any history of injuries.

Wear the socks and orthotics or other supports you expect to use when you run. And always bear your full weight on your foot when you check a shoe's fit. Look for a heel counter that wraps snugly around the back of your foot without pinching anywhere. If the heel feels too tight or too wide, try another shoe.

You should have a space that's at least as wide as a forefinger between your longest toe and the front of the shoe. If one foot is bigger than the other (as is the case with most people), buy shoes to fit the larger foot. Feet expand under the stress of running. Shoes that are a little tight around your forefoot in the store can be very uncomfortable on the jogging path.

Don't let anyone tell you what feels good, and don't depend on a "breaking in" period to make the shoes comfortable. Walk around the store to see how the shoes move. If you don't feel too silly, jog around the store. In fact, if the salesperson is agreeable, take the shoes for a test run around the block.

Safety Gates *(see Child's Safety Gates)*

SAILBOARDING

Sailboarding is basically a safe sport, if only because novices usually fall off before things get too rough. Beginners, though, should heed some commonsense safety advice.

Sailboarding lessons should be part of anyone's initial investment in the sport. With lessons, not only do you learn the basics of sailing but also how to avoid trouble once you're under way: what to do if the wind or tide carries a boarder too far from shore, what to do in a fall if there's no one close enough to help. Lessons should also include self-rescue technique—derigging the sail, laying it atop the board, and paddling back to shore. That strategy will help the boarder to cope with sudden overwhelming winds.

Beginners should wear a personal flotation device (life jacket). A vestlike Type III jacket should be adequate.

A safety leash to tether the sail rig to the board is an essential piece of equipment. It will prevent the board from being blown away in the event the rider falls off.

According to conventional wisdom, boarders should wear a neoprene wet suit if air and water temperatures drop much below 70° F. But even at 70° F or above, an unprotected body loses its heat rapidly because of a combination of exertion, wind, and repeated dunkings.

SALAD DRESSINGS

The classic French and Italian dressings are vinaigrettes—sauces based on oil and vinegar, plus various herbs and spices that give each dressing its special character. In a French dressing, those extras typically include salt, pepper, mustard, and onion; in an Italian dressing, they're a bolder array that includes basil, oregano, and garlic.

In America, however, the classic recipes have gone through some changes. "French" dressings usually contain tomato, which alters the flavor and color considerably. And "Italian" dressings often come in "creamy" versions that may or may not contain dairy products.

The following recipes are for the two classic dressings and include appropriate aromas and flavors at the intensities some consider ideal. The homemade French dressing has a moderate but not biting flavor and aroma of vinegar and onion, as well as a slight sourness and a hint of bitterness. The flavors are well blended so that no one of them dominates, and the dressing is devoid of gumminess. The recipe for Italian dressing is also of the classic variety. It has a moderate level of the flavors and aromas of garlic and Italian herbs, a mild bite of vinegar, and a touch of sourness.

Nutrition. The nutrients that a salad provides come mostly from the greens, not from the dressing. It's no surprise, then, that only a few commercial dressings carry nutritional labeling.

Salad dressing's chief contributions to the daily diet are fat and calories. The fat is generally from vegetable oil, so most of it should be unsaturated (the good kind). The oil supplies most of the calories; remove it and you get a reduced-calorie dressing.

The calorie content of dressings range from nearly 100 calories per tablespoon (for the homemade recipes and a few commercial products) downward. Products with 40 calories or less are marketed as reduced- or low-calorie dressings.

Salad dressings (especially Italian) tend to be high in sodium content. In fact, a single tablespoon of some of them would meet or exceed many people's daily salt requirement.

Classic French Dressing

¾	cup salad oil
2	tbsp water
2	tbsp white vinegar
1	tsp dry mustard
1	tsp sugar
½	tsp salt
½	tsp white pepper
1	tbsp ketchup
2	tsp finely chopped onion

After measuring out the oil and setting it aside, mix the water and vinegar in a cup and put that aside as well. Now combine the mustard, sugar, salt, pepper, and ketchup in a small bowl. Into that bowl, pour about a tablespoonful of the oil and then about ½ tablespoon of the water-vinegar mixture, beating with a wire whisk until the mixture is smooth and creamy. Continue beating while adding small amounts of the oil and the water-vinegar mixture alternately. Stir in the onion. Refrigerate any leftover dressing.

Yield: 1 cup.

Classic Italian Dressing

$1/2$	tsp dried basil
$1/2$	tsp dried oregano
$3/4$	tsp salt
$1/2$	tsp sugar
$1/4$	tsp pepper
$1/4$	tsp crushed garlic (1 medium clove)
3	tbsp red-wine vinegar
1	tbsp water
$3/4$	cup olive oil

Crumble the basil and oregano in the palm of your hand to release maximum flavor, then drop the crushed herbs into a jar, along with the salt, sugar, pepper, garlic, vinegar, and water. Cap the jar tightly and shake well. Now add the oil and shake again. Store the dressing in the refrigerator, but serve it at room temperature.

Yield: 1 cup.

SAVINGS ACCOUNTS

Here are some helpful tips when you shop for a savings account:

- *APR.* The Annual Percentage Rate is the basic yearly interest rate that the account pays.
- *Compounding.* The more frequent the compounding period, the better off you are. However, continuous compounding yields only a tiny bit more than daily compounding.
- *Yield.* The annual percentage yield takes into consideration both the APR and the frequency of compounding. It tells you by what percentage a deposit will grow if you leave it in the account for a full year.
- *Balance method.* How does the financial institution deter-

mine the amount on which interest is paid? The fairest method is called day of deposit to day of withdrawal (sometimes known as day in to day out, or DIDO). With it, you get interest each day on the actual balance in your account. Another common method is day of deposit to end of interest period. This means that withdrawals before the end of the interest period (usually the end of the month) don't earn interest for any of that period. The least equitable is the low-balance method. This system pays you interest only on the lowest balance in your account during the interest period, and ignores the rest.

• *Fees, charges, and penalties.* If your balance falls below a certain minimum, is there a service charge (or do you cease to earn interest)? Is there a charge for withdrawals after a certain number is reached? Is there a charge for so-called inactive accounts? What other special charges are there?

• *Delaying interest on deposits.* Does the financial institution start paying interest the day checks are deposited, or does it wait for the check to clear?

• *Deposit insurance.* Be sure to find out whether you would be covered by federal deposit insurance. Unless you have a basis to form an independent judgment on the adequacy of a state deposit-insurance fund, stick with a federally insured institution.

Shock (*see Electric Shock*)

Shoes (*see Running Shoes*)

SHOWER HEADS: LOW-FLOW

Bathing accounts for about 30 percent of the water a typical family uses. So if your family takes mostly showers, not baths, a low-flow shower head, which can cut the amount of water used in the shower by half, should reduce your water use by 15 percent or more. This savings is important if you live in an area that's drought-prone or where water is expensive. A low-flow shower head should also reduce your water-heating bill, since most of the water used for bathing is heated water.

Before you buy a low-flow shower head, you might want to try a cheaper alternative—a simple device called a *flow restrictor*. You can pick one up at a hardware store for about $2. A flow restrictor resembles a washer; it slips easily into the threaded fitting of the shower head. It will save water but, like some low-flow heads, may diminish the flow intensity more than you or your family may like.

SKIN MOISTURIZERS

Women are the prime target of moisturizer advertising, since they use far more moisturizers than men do. (Most men have thicker, oilier skin than women do, and they don't need moisturizers as much.)

Most women don't expect a moisturizing lotion to cure dry skin, just to soothe it and make it feel softer. In choosing an all-purpose moisturizer, ignore the ads for expensive products. A cheap, plain lotion is likely to do the best job.

The only way that you can soothe and soften dry skin is to restore the proper balance of moisture to the *stratum corneum*, the very top skin layer. A moisturizer helps do this in two ways.

First, most moisturizers contain some kind of oil, which helps retard the evaporation of water. Normally your skin produces enough oil on its own to form an adequate barrier. But various factors such as a harsh environment and soaps and detergents can strip the skin of its natural oils. Some people don't have much oil to begin with, having inherited a tendency toward dry skin. And oil production tends to slow down with age.

Moisturizers also work with the help of humectants—ingredients that attract and hold water as it passes through the *stratum corneum*. Humectants (glycerin is one) can also attract water from the air, but this works best in a humid environment, when you need a moisturizer least.

Because the main objective of moisturizing is to get and keep water in contact with the skin, the best time to apply a moisturizer is immediately after a shower or bath, while your skin is still damp.

Any effect a moisturizer has is only temporary, since it works only on the surface of the skin, smoothing, softening, and plumping up the dead cells. The truth is that no matter how expensive a moisturizer is, and no matter what special ingredients it contains, it won't "penetrate deeply" into skin layers, "nourish" the skin or "cure" dry skin. Let's look at some of the more popular ingredients.

Collagen and Elastin. Collagen is a protein substance found in connective tissue, cartilage, and bone. The dermis, which forms up to 85 percent of the thickness of skin, consists mainly of interlaced collagen fibers. Elastin, which is responsible for making the skin supple and flexible, consists of springlike fibers that run between the collagen fibers. When you are young, collagen and elastin fibers form a tight-knit network. But as you age, those fibers tend to deteriorate.

Unfortunately, you can't send your skin collagen reinforcements by smearing on a cream that contains new collagen fibers. Collagen and elastin molecules are just too big to penetrate the skin's top layer.

This is not to say these ingredients don't do anything for you. Both collagen and elastin are good at binding moisture to the skin's outer layer, especially at low humidity. And they have the added benefit of giving moisturizing creams and lotions a satiny feel.

Lanolin and Petrolatum. Lanolin is wool fat secreted from the oil glands of sheep. Petrolatum is just another name for petroleum jelly. Used as a component in a moisturizer, lanolin smooths and softens the skin. Lanolin also makes a cream more spreadable and helps it adhere better to the skin. Petroleum jelly has long been a favorite to apply to a baby's bottom because it's gentle and it forms a barrier to protect the skin from irritation. Plain petroleum jelly works as a moisturizer for adults, too. But it's greasy and it tends to rub off on clothes.

Cocoa Butter. This solid fat is from the roasted seeds of the cacao tree; the seeds are also the source of chocolate and cocoa. Cocoa butter is a useful ingredient in cosmetic products because it melts at room temperature. Like other oils, cocoa butter works by slowing the evaporation of moisture from the *stratum corneum.*

Aloe. An extract from the succulent plant *Aloe vera,* this substance is also a soothing and mild humectant. It can't nourish or rejuvenate the skin, however.

Vitamin E. This vitamin has been promoted as having special properties for the skin. But vitamin E works like other oils to set up a barrier to evaporation. One problem with vitamin E is that it is a potential allergen.

Sleepwear for Infants *(see Infants' Sleepwear)*

Soaps *(see Hand and Bath Soaps)*

SODIUM
If you have healthy kidneys, there's no known danger in restricting your sodium intake sharply over a long period. Normal kidney function enables the body to retain adequate stores of sodium even if your sodium intake is very low.

Everyone needs some sodium in the diet to replace routine losses, and about 200 milligrams a day is considered essential for survival. Since many foods contain sodium naturally, however, that minimum amount is easy to obtain without conscious effort. Diets containing less than 500 milligrams of sodium per day tend to be unpalatable for many people.

SOUPS

If you rely on commercially made soup for your daily lunch, you are making significant nutritional compromises. Soup alone doesn't contribute much toward your recommended daily nutritional requirements.

Each meal should provide approximately one-third of the U.S. Recommended Daily Allowance (U.S. RDA) for most nutrients. It's not possible to follow this rule strictly, and it's also impractical, if not boring. Protein missing from one meal can be made up in another. Breakfast alone can provide all the vitamin C needed for the day. And some nutrients, like vitamin A, needn't be eaten every day because the body can draw from its long-term stores.

But even allowing for a certain amount of dietary flexibility, commercial soups generally fall far short of needed nutrients. You can find this out for yourself, since most soup containers have the product's nutritional information right on the package or container.

Nutrition. Ready-to-serve chicken-noodle soups provide about 20 percent of the U.S. RDA for protein, and 15 percent of the U.S. RDA for niacin, probably because of the chicken content.

Many soups do offer more than 15 percent of the U.S. RDA for vitamin A. Yellow fruits and vegetables, such as tomatoes and carrots, are good sources of that vitamin.

The amount of calcium in most soups is negligible. But many New England chowders have close to 15 percent of the U.S. RDA, either from the milk already in them (frozen soups) or from the milk you add to them (canned soups).

Milk also contributes to a slightly higher protein level in these products.

Sodium. Like many highly processed foods, soups often contain large amounts of sodium—from about 700 to more than 1,000 milligrams per serving. Low-sodium soups have only 20 to 60 milligrams, but the saving in sodium exacts a toll in taste. On the other hand, you can season these soups to your taste rather than accept the manufacturer's judgment about what tastes good. And low-sodium soups are unlikely to contain monosodium glutamate (MSG), the flavor enhancer some folks may want to avoid.

"Hearty" or "home-style" soups generally contain more solids—noodles, vegetables, meat—than regular soups. Most regular soups contain approximately 1.5 to 2.5 ounces of solids per 8-ounce serving, while the chunky or home-style varieties usually have at least 3 ounces. The amount of expensive protein ingredients, however—beef pieces in vegetable-beef soup, chicken pieces in chicken-noodle, clams in chowder—is less than an ounce per serving, whether the soup is regular or chunky.

To make soup better food, augment it with other foods. Add a tuna sandwich and a glass of low-fat or skim milk, and you have a nutritious lunch that's fairly low in calories.

If you are concerned about sodium, and like soup, your alternatives are to doctor up a low-sodium brand to make it more palatable or to cook your own, using herbs and spices that suit your palate.

SPACKLING COMPOUNDS
New lightweight spackling products make it easier to get good results when you patch an old wall. The newest compounds are full of air, not in frothy bubbles, but in tiny glass spheres that provide attractive new properties.

The lightweights compete mainly with two older formulations. *Powdered compounds* contain plaster of paris and other fillers; they have to be mixed carefully with water. *Pre-mixed, latex-based compounds* are ready for immediate application.

For very large holes, or areas subject to wear and tear (around wall switches, for example), you may want a tougher material than a lightweight compound. You're then best off with a powdered compound. Powders also do well in deep fills, and most are so hard that you may bend a nail as you hammer it into the patch. (Try drilling a pilot hole first.) Powdered products also store well if kept in a dry place. Puttylike premixed compounds tend to dry out and harden once their containers have been opened.

Spackling Alternatives. *Wallboard compound,* also known as *tape-joint compound* and *joint cement,* is a paste that's used to cover nailheads and taped joints in wallboard. It can serve for small spackling chores such as refilling hairline cracks. But the material is not an all-purpose patcher.

Plaster of paris can make a hard, quick-drying patch, but the product doesn't offer any real advantage over an ordinary spackling compound.

Patching plaster, like plaster of paris, is a gypsum product, but it has retarders to slow up drying. Patching plaster should take about 90 minutes to set, enough time to let you correct irregularities.

A homemade compound such as flour and water, or even oatmeal, was usable when paints were oil-based. They still can be, in a pinch, if you use an alkyd paint over them. They won't be satisfactory under latex paints.

SPAGHETTI SAUCE
An excellent spaghetti sauce should have a red to red-orange color and not look like tomato soup. You should be able to

see flecks of herbs and chunks of tomato. The sauce should have a moderately thick consistency, and there should be a distinct fresh-tomato flavor. The sauce should be somewhat spicy. Meat sauce should have some fresh-meat aroma and flavor, and a mushroom sauce should taste of mushrooms.

Nutrition. A meatless spaghetti sauce over pasta, sprinkled with Parmesan cheese and served with a salad, is a relatively nutritious main meal that's not especially high in calories. Such a meal provides about one-third of a person's recommended daily allowance for various nutrients, including protein. And it contains much less fat and more carbohydrate than a meal of beef, potatoes, and a green vegetable. A ¾-cup serving of an average meatless sauce contains about 145 calories, 3 grams of protein, 5 grams of fat, and 21 grams of carbohydrate.

The following recipes for homemade sauces are lower in fat than most commercial products, and lower in calories, too, at about 105 per serving. You can make the basic recipe plain or liven it up with mushrooms or meat. If you like a spicier sauce, try the marinara recipe. Both recipes yield 6 ¾-cup servings.

Basic Spaghetti Sauce

3	tbsp olive oil
1	28-oz can concentrated crushed tomatoes
1	15-oz can tomato sauce
1	tbsp minced dehydrated onion
½	tsp minced dehydrated garlic
½	tsp dried basil
¼	tsp black pepper
1	tsp dried oregano
½	tsp dried parsley

Heat the olive oil in a 6-quart saucepan over medium heat. Add the crushed tomatoes and tomato sauce. Add the remaining ingredients. Blend in thoroughly. Simmer for 30 minutes over low heat, stirring often.

For mushroom sauce, sauté one drained 4½-ounce jar of mushrooms in the olive oil. Continue as for the basic sauce.

For meat sauce, brown ½ pound of ground beef in a pan. Drain off the fat; add to basic sauce during the last 10 minutes of simmering.

Marinara Sauce

3	tbsp olive oil
1	small onion, chopped
1	celery stalk, chopped
½	medium green pepper, chopped
1	28-oz can whole tomatoes in sauce
1	15-oz can tomato sauce
½	tsp minced dehydrated garlic
½	tsp dried basil
¼	tsp black pepper
1	tsp dried oregano
½	tsp dried parsley

Heat the olive oil in a 6-quart saucepan over medium heat. Add the fresh onion, celery, and green pepper, and sauté until transparent. Add the tomato products and stir thoroughly. Add the remaining ingredients. Simmer the sauce for 30 minutes, stirring frequently.

Stains (see House Paints and Stains)

Steamers *(see Irons: Travel Irons and Steamers)*

Stoves *(see Ranges)*

STRAWBERRY JAM AND PRESERVES

Strawberry jam should taste and smell like real strawberries. But some of the flavor of the fresh berry is lost even when you put up preserves in the old-fashioned way, by cooking the fresh fruit with sugar and pouring it into jars.

When you start with frozen fruit, as the commercial makers usually do, much more of the fresh berry flavor is lost. A commercial strawberry jam, then, can't be expected to match a good homemade jam. Still, it should capture as much of the aroma and flavor of the berries as possible.

A quality jam should be sweet, but not *overwhelmingly* sweet. It may or may not contain large pieces of strawberries. The fruit pieces in jams should be relatively firm, and the gel around the fruit should be soft yet cohesive. The jam should be easy to spread.

Calories. Jam is usually 60 to 65 percent sugars, the level that retards spoilage. This much sugar translates into lots of calories, about 65 calories per 1-tablespoon serving.

Low-calorie jam uses less sugar, or sometimes substitutes saccharin, so it may contain only about 28 calories per tablespoon. Instead of using a lot of sugar to prevent spoilage, low-calorie jam contains preservatives, such as ascorbic acid (vitamin C), sorbates, and propionates, all of which are considered safe to eat.

STRING TRIMMERS

A string trimmer uses a rapidly spinning plastic line to cut grass and weeds at lawn edges, around trees and shrubs, and other places you can't reach with a lawn mower. As the string becomes worn, you can renew it from a spool in a central hub.

Many smaller models can cut swaths no wider than about 7 or 8 inches. However, a good gasoline-powered model can scythe down a swath 15 to 17 inches wide. But a trimmer won't leave large areas well manicured—its cutting action is less well controlled than a lawn mower's.

Some trimmers have two cutting strings instead of one. Although two strings do a slightly neater job of trimming fine grass, the differences between one- and two-string models are insignificant for most cutting tasks.

Gas versus Electric. If you have an acre of land or more, with the outskirts several hundred feet from an electrical outlet, an electric trimmer will be inadequate. But if your landscaping responsibilities end close to the house and near an outlet, a gasoline-powered trimmer is overqualified. If *either* power source seems appropriate for your needs, your choice really hinges on the kind of machine you would find easier to put up with. Would you rather manage a trailing power cord or pamper a fussy little gasoline engine? Gasoline-powered trimmers are more powerful but can be hard to start. They're susceptible to flooding and may be reluctant to fire up after they have been sitting in the sun.

String Feed. Most trimmers pay out new string on command, with a "bump" feed that releases new string every time you bump the cutting head on the ground. A bump feed can work well, although it may encourage you to waste string by the ease with which you can bump fresh string into action.

Avoid the older-design "slide bump" heads in which the entire head slides up and down on an exposed shaft. After a while the shaft can become choked with a tangle of grass and weeds, which will prevent the head from sliding on the shaft.

Safety. The whirling string in a trimmer won't inflict the terrible injuries that can come from the metal blades of lawn mowers. But a trimmer is capable of hurling debris in the eyes and cutting bare skin. So it's a good idea to wear goggles, long pants, and lace-up shoes rather than loafers or sandals when you use it.

More than that, though, you should have a way to stop the string quickly. You can do this with an electric trimmer by simply releasing the trigger. A gasoline engine should drop to idle speed and slow the string when you release the throttle. Look for a model that has a clutch, which can stop the string without stopping the engine. In an emergency, an engine-kill switch near your thumb lets you stop the engine quickly.

A gasoline trimmer with a fuel-filler opening below the engine is more convenient than one higher up. With a top-or-side-fill tank, it's all too easy to spill fuel on a hot engine, and risk a fire.

SUNSCREENS AND SUNBURN

A tan may be fashionable, but the unpleasant truth is that sunlight damages your skin—whether or not you suffer a sunburn. Ultraviolet radiation from the sun damages the elastin fibers in the skin, causing the sagging, wrinkling, and generally weather-beaten look associated with years of excessive sun exposure. The damage is cumulative; signs of overexposure may not show up for 20 or 30 years. But the damage is irreversible.

Overexposure can also cause skin cancer, the most common form of cancer in the United States. One in 7 Americans will develop skin cancer, and 90 percent of the cases are due to overexposure to the sun.

Unfortunately, you can't always tell when you've had too

much sun until it's too late. Sunburn doesn't appear until about 2 hours after sun exposure, and it takes 16 to 24 hours for the symptoms to reach their peak.

Despite well-documented dangers, the sun's emanations continue to have enormous appeal for many Americans. Fortunately, pharmaceutical and cosmetics manufacturers—and sometimes nature—have been able to come up with protective products that can help to ameliorate the problem.

To protect against ultraviolet radiation that damages skin even as it tans it, the body produces melanin, a skin pigment that migrates to the uppermost layers of the skin from the layers deep within, where it is manufactured. The darker your complexion, the more melanin and natural protection you have—though even the darkest-skinned people can burn if their exposure is severe enough.

Most of the sun's effect on the skin is caused by a type of ultraviolet radiation called ultraviolet-B (UV-B). Another type, ultraviolet-A (UV-A), can cause photosensitive skin reactions in people taking certain drugs and can cause cataracts over time. For this reason, the use of sunglasses while outdoors in the sun is strongly recommended.

Short of staying out of the sun altogether, the best way to protect your skin against the potential damage of the sun's rays is to use a sunscreen product having a high sun-protection factor (SPF). The SPF indicates a multiple of the time it takes the sun to produce a certain effect on your skin. A person who can stay in the sun for just 30 minutes without burning will be protected for 60 minutes with an SPF 2 sunscreen or for 10 hours with an SPF 20 sunscreen. Compared with low-SPF sunscreens, the higher SPF products have both a greater number of screening chemicals and more of each chemical. Most sunscreens are formulated to filter both UV-A and UV-B.

The label on a container of sunscreen can tell you a lot:

- *Waterproof* means that the product will protect you at the labeled SPF value even after four 20-minute swims. A *water-resistant* product is supposed to retain its SPF through two such swims. The manufacturer's claims are likely to be reliable.

- *Clear lotion* is better described as a liquid. It's a clear, alcohol-based product that leaves a thin, noticeable film on your skin when it dries. But the product isn't greasy: sand won't stick to it.

- *Highest level of protection* is a term that may be loosely used by marketers. Although SPF 15 can be considered to be virtually a total sun block in most of the continental United States, you can easily find products with SPFs in the 20s and 30s to take with you to the tropics.

- *The Skin Cancer Foundation* is a nonprofit educational group whose acceptance seal appears on some sunscreens. The seal shows that the product has an SPF of at least 15 and is waterproof or water-resistant.

- *Sunscreen chemicals* are potent. Many of them, especially PABA (para-aminobenzoic acid) and PABA derivatives (which have almost entirely replaced pure PABA) can irritate some people's skin. If a sunscreen makes skin red or itchy, stop using it and switch to a brand that uses different active ingredients.

Tanning. How well you tan and how much you can tolerate before burning depends on your genes. Some 15 percent of the white population falls into the category that must use a sunscreen providing total or nearly total protection.

People with a light to medium complexion, who burn only moderately and tan to a light brown, should be fully protected from a sunburn with a sunscreen of SPF 4 to 6. Dark-skinned people should be able to get by with a sunscreen of SPF 2, or no sunscreen at all.

Ultraviolet rays don't feel hot, so it's easy to be fooled if there's a cool breeze or overcast skies. Nor is shade or thin clothing a good barrier: ultraviolet radiation can reflect off sand and water, pass through gauzy robes and wet T-shirts, and penetrate several feet underwater.

As you become more tan, you can gradually decrease the SPF number on the sunscreen you use. It takes about 2 weeks for the average person to develop a tan.

SWEETENERS

Concerned about weight control and fearful of obesity, Americans have turned in increasing numbers to diet foods and beverages made with low-calorie artificial sweeteners. Sugars such as sucrose and corn sweeteners are equivalent in calorie content. As for artificial sweeteners, some authorities suggest that when these substances are used for weight control, people tend to increase their consumption of other foods, leaving their total calorie intake roughly unchanged or even increased. Still, many people crave an alternative to sugar. Here's a quick look at what's known—and not known—about sugar and each of the major alternatives:

Sugar. A teaspoon of sugar contains 16 calories, a can of sugar-sweetened soda, about 160. If you are trying to lose weight, sugar is only part of the picture. Fats contain 9 calories per gram, compared with 4 for carbohydrates, including sugar. Sugar that clings to the teeth—such as candy, honey, or granulated sugar—is more likely to promote tooth decay than the liquid forms, such as sugared beverages.

Saccharin. This calorie-free compound, 300 times sweeter than sugar, has been shown to promote cancer in laboratory animals. The sole U.S. maker of saccharin has noted that people have been using saccharin for most of a century with no clear indication of ill effects. However, this doesn't necessarily mean that saccharin is safe for human consumption.

Opponents of saccharin point out that consumption of artificial sweetners was relatively low until the past decade or two and that many forms of cancer have a long latency period.

Aspartame. Aspartame has the same number of calories as sugar, weight for weight. However, since it is 200 times sweeter than sugar, it contributes only 1/200th as many calories to the diet. Some aspartame products use glucose, a sugar, as a carrier for the aspartame. This adds a few calories, but the total remains lower than in an equivalent portion of sugar.

Although some questions remain about aspartame's safety and the soundness of the process that led to its approval, the substance seems to be acceptably safe for most people when used in moderation.

Phenylalanine, an amino acid, is one of the two components of aspartame. As a result, aspartame may pose a risk to people who suffer from the metabolic disorder called phenylketonuria (PKU). But even to PKU patients, aspartame has been judged to pose only a small risk. There is a substantial safety factor in the difference between the blood levels of phenylalanine that could occur in heavy users of aspartame and the lowest known toxic levels for PKU patients.

As for other side effects, the U.S. Centers for Disease Control's position has been that while some people may be unusually sensitive to aspartame, the data "do not provide evidence for the existence of serious, widespread, adverse health consequences." The Council on Scientific Affairs of the American Medical Association (AMA) also went on record, in mid-1985, stating: "Available evidence suggests that consumption of aspartame by normal humans is safe and is not associated with serious adverse health effects. Individuals who need to control their phenylalanine intake should handle aspartame like any other source of phenylalanine."

Sorbitol. This sweetener, and its close relative, mannitol, is used in sugar-free candies, mints, chewing gum, and the like. Sorbitol, found naturally in some fruits and berries, has the same number of calories per gram as ordinary table sugar but is only about half as sweet. Unlike sugar, however, sorbitol does not promote dental cavities. Sorbitol is digested slowly, so it is used in some foods for diabetics and in certain "low-sugar" gums and candies.

Some people are troubled by excess gas and diarrhea after consuming sorbitol or mannitol.

TANNING SALONS

Tanning salons promote the idea that the equipment they use reduces or eliminates "harmful" ultraviolet-B (UV-B) rays and steps up the output of "safe" ultraviolet-A (UV-A) rays. Actually, both types of rays cause the skin to tan, but UV-B is much more apt to cause sunburn.

In 1985, the American Medical Association (AMA) issued a report that warned of many possible dangers from the use of sun lamps. "Many people, particularly young people, who are doing this are going to have significant problems," said Dr. Paul Lazar, professor of clinical dermatology at Northwestern University Medical School and an author of the AMA report.

Dr. Lazar and other dermatologists are not reassured by the tanning salons' switch to UV-A. Sunburn, they pointed out, is only one of several potential dangers. UV-A, which penetrates more deeply into the skin, can produce the wrinkled, leathery look of prematurely aged skin. Sunlight, in particular the ultraviolet portion of the sun's rays, is a well-established risk factor in skin cancer. While UV-B is the most carcinogenic fraction of the spectrum, some studies indicate that UV-A can harm the cornea and lens of the eye, and repeated exposure to either UV-A or UV-B may cause cataracts.

Dr. Lazar also noted that UV-B provides a "biological marker." When you get a sunburn, he said, "you know you've had enough." But with UV-A, you don't have any warning signal.

TEAS

All teas sold in America are blends, usually of black Indian or Ceylon teas. The "orange pekoe" or "pekoe" on the label merely indicates the size of the leaf, not the name of the tea. The common English brands offer a variety of black-tea blends labeled English Breakfast or Irish Breakfast (which mean nothing in themselves) or Darjeeling, which refers to one variety of black Indian tea used in the blend. Some of these imports are marketed at double, triple, even quadruple the price of U.S. packaged tea.

Taste. An excellent black tea should be full-bodied. It should not be flat-tasting but should have the character that tasters call "brisk" or "lively"—the tea should tingle on the tongue. It should also have some pungency and bitterness. It may contain floral or malty notes—sometimes both. (Maltiness refers to the actual aroma and flavor of the malt, which can be described as cooked, sweetish, and slightly reminiscent of caramel.) An excellent tea should have no off-flavors, such as notes of wood, weeds, hay, or fermented fruit. Unless it's a smoky tea, it should have no smoke notes.

Caffeine. The amount of caffeine in tea can vary widely, depending on the type of tea leaves used and the strength of the brew. The longer the tea is steeped, the more caffeine.

Black tea contains an average of about 60 milligrams of caffeine per tea bag—about half of what you get in a cup of coffee. (And a cup of *weak* tea might provide only one-fourth the caffeine of coffee.) Loose teas tend to contain less caffeine than do tea bags.

If you are sensitive to caffeine, try a decaffeinated black

tea. Its caffeine content has been sharply reduced, possibly to one-third or less of that in a regular tea.

Herbal Tea. Early herbal-tea elixirs, made of herbs collected from the woods and fields, were first used as medicines. By the time herbal teas came into health-food stores, they had become more of a soothing drink, a mild and caffeine-free alternative to coffee or black tea.

The best herbal or flavored tea is the one that tastes best to you.

TELEPHONE ANSWERING MACHINES

In less than a dozen years, the answering machine has gone from exotic oddity to fairly ordinary household tool. As the answering machine has evolved, it's become friendlier.

Early models took only a short message, often hanging up on a verbose caller in midsentence. Now virtually all models have VOX, or voice-sensing circuitry. It detects when callers are speaking and when they've stopped, so callers can talk as much or as little as they wish.

Which answering machine to buy depends on how you intend to use it. People who get lots of calls will lean toward machines that can hold lots of messages. People who need to retrieve messages while on the road will prefer machines with the most convenient remote-control capabilities. Those who want an all-in-one unit will look for an answerer/telephone combination, perhaps one with a speakerphone or a two-line unit. And people with an outdated model may be tempted to replace it with one that offers VOX and a beeperless remote.

Repairs. An industry report estimates an answering machine's average life expectancy at about 5 years, and a recent reader survey found that 1 in 10 owners needed to have their machine repaired in the last 3 years. Many of the models only have a 1-year warranty, but some do offer better deals.

TELEPHONE FRAUD

Each year, high-pressure telephone salespeople cheat consumers in a big way. Con artists promote precious metals, rare coins, stamps, currency contracts, oil and gas leases, artwork—anything a trusting investor is willing to buy. If you think you have been victimized by an unscrupulous salesperson, or if you are considering an investment with an unfamiliar firm, contact the following authorities for help and advice:

- *Commodities Futures Trading Commission (CFTC)*. To find out if the CFTC has filed any litigation against a company, call 202-254-8630. To file a complaint against a futures company, or to find out if there have been other consumer complaints, call the CFTC at 202-254-3060.
- *Federal Trade Commission (FTC)*. To find out if action has been taken against a company by the FTC, or to file a complaint, call 202-326-2222.
- *National Association of Securities Dealers (NASD)*. For additional information on a securities firm, call the NASD at 301-738-6500.
- *National Futures Association (NFA)*. All futures companies trading on the futures exhange must be registered. To find out if a commodities company is registered, call the NFA at 800-621-3570. Just because a company is registered doesn't mean it's necessarily legitimate, so investigate further before investing.
- *Securities and Exchange Commission (SEC)*. To find out if action has been taken against a particular company by the SEC, call 202-272-7440.
- *State and local authorities*. Before investing, consider contacting the Better Business Bureau in your state and in the state where the offer was first made.

TELEPHONES

Today, the telephone has merged with other devices—computers, facsimile machines, and particularly with answering machines. The product that has resulted is called, in the language of the trade, an "integrated telephone answering device."

This fast pace of change complicates shopping, however. Packages and ads spell out features incompletely or incoherently. Sales staff often can't explain the product, either.

Before you rush out to buy a phone loaded with features, ask yourself whether you really need all the electronic talents that come with a top-of-the-line model. The 32-number memory bank and speakerphone that are so useful at the office may be silly to have on a bedside phone and excessive even for a study desk. A traditional no-frills model for desk or wall lists for about $50 and may be found on sale for less. You can find small phones selling for much less—of uncertain quality, perhaps, but worth considering as a spare.

Here are some other considerations:

• There are features for special needs in today's phones—compatibility with hearing aids, lighted buttons, volume that can be turned up or down. Ask your dealer for information on these types of accessories.

• Try holding the receiver to your ear before you make a final decision to buy. A poorly shaped earpiece can make the phone painful to press against the ear.

• Whichever model you buy, be sure you can return it if it doesn't work on your line.

TELEPHONES: CORDLESS

Despite its many conveniences, a cordless phone may not deliver the voice quality you may be accustomed to with a conventional phone. And background noise can also be intrusive.

The batteries can quit unexpectedly, and most won't operate at all when there's a power blackout, since their base station needs household electricity. A cordless phone is expensive; even at discount, you should expect to pay two to three times as much as you would for a good corded phone.

Nevertheless, you may still feel that a cordless phone's convenience far outweighs its possible shortcomings. For people with big houses and for those who have trouble getting around, a cordless phone can be a boon. The phones also make easy-to-install extensions for rooms without telephone wiring. Furthermore, new technology and additional channels have improved the cordless phones made in the last few years.

TELEVISION SETS

Buying a television set today is a matter of making choices—lots of them. Here are some features to look for:

Sound. When you buy your next color TV set, give first consideration to a model that has stereo-sound capability. You're also likely to get a set that delivers good picture quality and very good sound in both the stereo and monophonic modes.

Stereo sets are at the high end of the price spectrum and typically include input and output jacks for such peripheral equipment as a stereo videocassette recorder and a high-fidelity sound system. Less expensive sets are a lot simpler, with monophonic sound, fewer accessory jacks, and, in some cases, a less deluxe remote control.

Channel Selector. The old-fashioned rotary knob tuner is found only on the cheapest sets. Higher-priced models generally have some sort of electronic selector that gives you "direct access": you can go directly from channel 2 to channel 9, for example.

One type of electronic tuner rarely found in the more expensive models involves the tedious setting of tiny buttons, dials, or switches to bring in the desired channels. Once these controls have been set, you change channels with a button or a knob. Some tuners limit the number of channels you can receive at one time—which is an annoyance to cable-TV users who have two dozen or more channels available. Quartz-locked tuners are best in this respect because they can receive many more of the available channels.

Remote Control. This feature is practically standard with most TVs. On some sets, the remote control is a necessity because some tuning, sound, and picture controls are only on the remote, and not on the TV set.

Displays. A lot of sets display the channel you are watching—or the time of day—on the TV screen at the touch of a button. The clock feature can be a nuisance if a power interruption wipes out the set's timekeeping memory, making it necessary to reprogram the gadget. Better sets use the display in a menulike fashion to indicate and select the set's picture and connection options, such as Color, Sound, VCR, etc.

Auxiliary Inputs and Outputs. A TV set designed specifically to serve as the command center of an entire home-entertainment system can offer a number of conveniences:

- An *audio output jack* lets you shut off sound from the TV set's speakers and route it directly to a hi-fi system. The jack also allows a connection to an audio tape recorder, so that you can record sound tracks or televised music programs.
- *Video and audio input jacks* allow you to leave a component such as a videocassette recorder or a computer permanently connected while providing a slightly clearer picture than you could get with a connection through the TV set's antenna terminals.
- An *S-VHS connection* is usually included in better sets to allow the connection of an S-VHS videocassette recorder.
- An *earphone jack*, called a *muting jack*, lets you hear a program without annoying others. You need a *nonmuting jack* to

pipe sound directly to the ear of someone who is hard of hearing without cutting off sound to the rest of the family. Some sets have both types.

• *The connection to cable.* A set advertised as "cable ready" can receive at least 23 channels reserved for nonscrambled cable programs, with no need for the cable company's converter box. You *will* need a converter box if the signal is delivered scrambled. And you'll need an *addressable decoder* to watch pay-per-view programs.

When you are tied in to cable you may find that you can't make full use of your videocassette recorder without getting some extra hardware. You may not, for example, be able to watch one program while recording another.

Screens. The smallest sets are pocket-size, black-and-white or color. Sold as novelties, they are expensive.

As for consoles and table models, the bigger the screen, the higher the cost. Prices may start as low as about $45 for a 12-inch black-and-white set.

Some sets have a flat-faced, squared-off picture tube. Since picture dimensions are measured on the diagonal, the square corners add an extra inch or so to the screen. (A 19-inch set becomes a 20-inch model when the tube is square.)

A set with a 19- or 20-inch screen is large enough for the whole family to watch yet small enough so that it won't dominate the room.

You may want to consider a set with a 35-inch "direct-view" screen or a projection TV set if you have a particularly big viewing room or if you want to approach the big-screen impact of a movie theater. But be prepared to spend a few thousand dollars.

THERMOMETERS: FEVER

The traditional mercury-and-glass thermometer is giving way to the microprocessor and liquid crystal display (LCD). These new digital thermometers rely on electrical measurements monitored by a tiny computer chip. Safer than breakable glass thermometers, they are also easier to use. Temperature registers in clear figures on a display similar to that on a digital wristwatch. You don't have to shake down a digital thermometer, and it gives readings in a fraction of the time a glass thermometer takes—and often signals with a "beep" when it's ready to be read.

Most digital models come with a supply of sanitary *probe covers*, disposable plastic sheaths that fit over the thermometer's tip. These covers are potentially hazardous to young children—they can cause choking if swallowed or inhaled. Instead of using them, clean the probe end of a digital thermometer with soap and lukewarm water or with rubbing alcohol. Don't immerse a digital thermometer completely or splash water on the readout, which could ruin it.

THERMOMETERS: MEAT

You can always cook roasts and fowl by sheer guesswork, but you'll get more satisfactory results if you use a meat thermometer. The trick to using a meat thermometer is to insert its sensitive tip more or less into the center of the thickest part of your roast or poultry, but well clear of any bones, masses of gristle or fat, or air spaces.

If you insist on stuffing your poultry, insert the meat thermometer in the middle of the stuffing, especially if it's a raw pork-sausage stuffing. The temperature should reach 140°F to ensure complete cooking of the stuffing. Unfortunately, by the time the interior of the stuffing reaches the optimum heat, other parts of the bird might be overcooked. For ultimate safety, bake the stuffing separately. It will be less soggy and taste better, too.

Pork and some game meats demand special attention because of the possibility that they might contain *Trichinella spiralis*, the parasitic worm that causes trichinosis. Authorities used to recommend that fresh pork be cooked to 185°F, to be sure that any parasites are rendered harmless. More recently, studies have demonstrated that an interior temperature of 170°F is hot enough to make pork safe. Some thermometers may still carry the old 185°F recommendation; others recommend the lower temperature.

THERMOMETERS: OVEN
If recipes have been taking longer or shorter times to cook than they ought to, consider buying and using an oven thermometer.

Put the thermometer as near the center of the oven as possible. Set the oven for the temperature you use most often and let it run for at least 15 minutes. Take a reading and record the temperature. Take several additional readings at 10- to 15-minute intervals, then average the results. Compare the average with the thermostat setting. If the oven temperature is incorrect, you can make a mark on the thermostat dial to remind yourself to set the oven higher or lower than the dial indicates. Or you may prefer to call a service technician to recalibrate the oven, or do the job yourself if the manufacturer's instructions are available.

If you often cook using both top and bottom shelves of the oven, you may want to check the temperatures in both places. It's common to find a considerable difference in temperature between the two. If the two readings aren't the same, there isn't much you can do about it except change cooking times to compensate for the difference.

Mercury Thermometer. When shopping, you'll find both dial and mercury-in-glass models. A mercury model generally offers very accurate readings. But the mercury can pose a health hazard if the thermometer breaks and spills. Although a metal-encased mercury thermometer might be hard to break even when accidentally dropped, it would pose a special hazard if left in the oven during a self-cleaning cycle. In such a hot oven, the thermometer is likely to burst, and the mercury will vaporize. Mercury vapor is highly toxic. Even at room temperature, spilled mercury is a hazard.

Should a mercury thermometer ever break, sweep the mercury into a dustpan, if possible, or pick up as much as you can with an eyedropper. Do *not* use a vacuum cleaner—it will vaporize the mercury and spread it through the room air. Place the collected mercury in a jar or bottle with a lid, and throw it away. Air the room thoroughly.

TICK-BORNE DISEASES

In 1976, Dr. Allen Steere of the Yale Medical School reported a "new" disease. He dubbed it *Lyme arthritis*, after the Connecticut town where a cluster of children with juvenile rheumatoid arthritis (a rare disorder) had been discovered. Subsequent research established the relationship between the symptoms and the bite of the deer tick.

In the Northeast, where most Lyme disease cases occur, adult ticks feed and mate on deer, then drop off to lay their eggs. The eggs hatch into deer-tick larvae, which contract the infection by feeding on the white-footed mouse, the primary carrier of the Lyme disease spirochete. The larvae eventually molt into infected "nymphs," an adolescent stage of tick development that poses the chief threat to humans.

Nymphs are active in late spring and summer, when people tend to be outdoors more. They are also much smaller than adult ticks and are thus harder to spot on clothing or skin. Most people who contract Lyme disease have been bitten by nymphs. Nymphs readily latch on to ground-feeding birds as well—which is thought to be how the disease spreads to distant areas.

While ticks transmit several other diseases, most occur only in specific localities and far less frequently than Lyme disease. *Babesiosis*, for example, which produces headache, fever, and chills, tends to affect about a dozen people each year, mainly in the Cape Cod, Massachusetts, area and on the eastern end of Long Island in New York State. *Colorado tick fever*, which affects an estimated 50 to 150 people annually, is similarly regional and occurs only among those who live or work at altitudes above 4,000 feet.

An exception to the localized pattern is *Rocky Mountain spotted fever*, which was reported in 40 states in 1986. Of 775 cases reported in 1986, nearly half occurred in the Southeast, especially in the Carolinas. Oklahoma was also hard-hit, with 104 cases.

Rocky Mountain spotted fever can sometimes be fatal—it killed 23 people in the United States in 1986. The infecting agent, a microbe from a group called *rickettsia*, is transmitted by the Rocky Mountain wood tick in the West and the American dog tick in the East.

Nearly all cases of Rocky Mountain spotted fever occur in the spring and summer, generally several days after exposure to infected ticks. The onset of illness is abrupt, often with high fever, headache, chills, and severe weakness. By about the fourth day of fever, victims may develop a spotted pink rash, which usually starts on the hands and feet and gradually extends to most of the body.

As with Lyme disease, early detection and treatment significantly reduces the severity of the illness.

Prevention. In areas where tick-borne disease exists, it makes sense to take certain precautions—whether you're hiking in the woods or just spending time in the backyard.

• Don't go out barefoot or in open sandals. Do wear long pants. Cinching pants at the ankle or tucking them into boots or socks gives added protection, since ticks lie low, on grass blades and shrubs. They attach themselves to your feet, ankles, or lower legs and then crawl upward. Keep them on the outside of your clothing, not inside.

• Wear light-colored clothing outdoors (this makes ticks easier to spot) and check your clothes every so often. Be especially careful in terrain with tall grass, bushes, or woods. Try to stay in the middle of trails to avoid contact with tick-bearing bushes.

• Use a tick repellent, especially if you spend a lot of time outdoors. (*See* Insect Repellents.)

• With children, start a bedtime check for ticks from about mid-April through September. Tick-borne disease affects people of all ages, but children are at special risk because they spend so much time outside.

• Check pets for ticks. If a pet brings ticks inside, you can get infected without ever leaving the house.

• Know what to look for when making a tick check. A biting deer tick rarely hurts enough to draw your attention. To find one you'll have to look for it—especially the tiny deer-tick nymph, which is smaller than a sesame seed. A nymph that's been attached to the skin for several hours looks like a blood blister with legs.

• Pregnant women should be especially careful. Lyme disease spirochetes can cross the placenta.

TIRE-PRESSURE GAUGES

Improperly inflated tires can cause poor handling, blowouts, even high-speed accidents.

Significantly underinflated tires can suffer from uneven, accelerated tread wear, as well as from excessive flexing, which causes overheating and may lead to early tire failure. Over-inflated tires also wear unevenly, give a harsher ride, and can cause handling problems or blowouts.

To maintain your tires properly, buy a good pencil-shaped

gauge. Get one for each car you own, keep it in the glove compartment, and use it once a month or so. It will safeguard the life of your tires and help ensure safe driving.

You can't rely on a gas station's air hose. The station's air dispenser may not be accurate. What's more, if you've driven any distance to the station, your tires will have warmed and therefore increased their pressure by as much as 4 to 6 pounds per square inch (psi).

The recommended pressure for your car's tires (the *maximum* pressure is embossed directly on the tire sidewall) is usually for cold readings. A tire gauge lets you read the pressure right in your own driveway. If tires are underinflated, you can then drive to the gas station and inflate each tire by the requisite number of pounds, using the tire gauge as the measuring instrument.

While you are checking, don't neglect the spare. Air slowly seeps through the pores of any tire. A spare sitting in the trunk can become so underinflated as to be useless.

TOASTER OVENS AND TOASTER-OVEN/BROILERS

A toaster oven and a toaster-oven/broiler are small appliances meant for small jobs. They should be able to save you the trouble of heating a full-size oven (and the kitchen, along with it) just to warm a little bit of food. They should also be easy to clean.

In addition to making toast, a toaster oven can heat a frozen dinner, bake potatoes or a small meat loaf, warm rolls, and do many of the chores a regular oven does, but on a smaller scale. A toaster-oven/broiler can do these baking chores and broil, too.

While toasting bread and rolls is by far the most common use for these appliances, an old-fashioned toaster is more effective at toasting bread.

A toaster-oven/broiler is more versatile than a toaster oven, and may cost no more, especially when you consider the big discounts you can often find for these products. A small toaster-oven/broiler is also handy for quick warm-ups when you want crispness rather than the steamy quality that a microwave oven provides. A skillet on a range top makes a better hamburger, but a toaster-oven/broiler is convenient, and it does a respectable job.

TOASTERS

Manufacturers have just about perfected toaster technology. You can expect most toaster models on the market to make toast to your liking.

Once the color control is set, a toaster should be able to produce batch after batch of toast to just the selected shade of brown. Later batches shouldn't be darker or lighter than earlier ones.

While not likely to win many design awards, the traditional pop-up toaster is functional. Most two-slice and four-slice models have slots just big enough for slices of supermarket bread, but there are some with extra-wide slots for bakery and frozen-food-case items that require the extra width.

The amount of toast you usually make at a single sitting and the amount of counter space in your kitchen will largely dictate whether you choose a two-slice or four-slice model. Convenience features—controls, handles, cord length, and the like—may also influence your decision.

The typical toast-color control is a sliding lever set below a series of numbers or a color scale that ranges from off-white to dark brown. The control on some toasters is a knob instead of a lever. The control is simple enough to use, and usually easy enough to reach and move.

The four-slice models that have their slots lined up side by side have two levers so you can toast two slices of bread without heating up all four elements. They also have two color controls so, if you're toasting four slices at once, you can make two light and two dark, if you wish.

TOOTHPASTES
Plaque is a soft, sticky bacterial film that coats teeth. If sufficient plaque accumulates on teeth and grows down into the crevices between teeth and gums, gum disease may be the result.

Plaque that isn't brushed away can combine with the minerals in saliva to form a calcified plaque called tartar or calculus. Tartar is a rock-hard, white or yellowish deposit that can only be "scaled" from teeth and from under gums during a professional cleaning.

Prevention. Regular and thorough brushing and flossing can usually remove almost all plaque and prevent tartar formation. Tartar builds mainly on those tooth surfaces most exposed to saliva, so extra brushing near the salivary glands— the tongue side of the lower front teeth and the cheek side of the upper back teeth—can prevent much of the buildup of tartar.

Toothpastes that make antitartar claims do contain effective antitartar ingredients. Unfortunately, they'll do nothing to dissolve the tartar that's already on your teeth; only a dentist or dental hygenist can get that off. Furthermore, the products inhibit tartar buildup only above the gum line; they can't head off tartar that forms where a toothbrush doesn't reach.

So, despite studies showing that tartar-inhibiting toothpastes may reduce the accumulation of new tartar by one-third or more, these products are strictly cosmetic and have no real consequence for total dental health.

Abrasiveness. To help remove plaque and stains, toothpastes all contain abrasives such as hydrated silica or phosphate salts. Toothpaste alone won't affect tooth enamel (the nonliving material that forms the visible crown of a tooth), because that enamel is the hardest substance in the human body. But when gums recede with age or disease, softer dental tissues become exposed. These tissues include dentin (cellular material below the enamel that forms the bulk of each tooth) and cementum (a bonelike material that helps anchor the tooth in place). Either can be damaged by a toothpaste that's too abrasive.

Use the least abrasive toothpaste that gets your teeth clean, especially if your gums have begun to recede. People with heavily stained teeth may require a more abrasive toothpaste, at least occasionally.

Fluoride. Another important factor in choosing a toothpaste is fluoride. A fluoride formula that has been shown to be effective can give everyone, regardless of age, added protection against cavities.

The American Dental Association (ADA) has a Council on Dental Therapeutics that requires manufacturers to submit rigorous research data demonstrating that the fluoride in a toothpaste actually works in preventing tooth decay.

TOY SAFETY

Parents should take a close look at rattles, squeeze toys, and other playthings for infants and toddlers. Toys that seem even remotely capable of being swallowed should be destroyed and discarded. Some experts believe that objects have to be 1¾ inches in diameter to be fully safe.

TUNA

What's the best tuna? Depending on what you're making, the best canned tuna may be the cheapest. If you plan to mix the tuna with mayonnaise and onion in a salad or with other ingredients in a casserole, any canned tuna should do.

If you want to eat tuna straight, you will probably be able to detect subtle differences between types and brands. You may prefer a moister oil-packed tuna. You may also prefer the milder taste of albacore to the stronger taste of light-meat tuna. If you do, you'll usually have to pay extra for it.

Low-salt brands are the highest-priced. If you are watching sodium intake, you can save money by buying regular tuna and rinsing it under running water. Rinsing the tuna may diminish the taste somewhat, but that shouldn't matter as much in a tuna salad.

Nutrition. Canned tuna is high in a number of important vitamins and minerals. Like most fish, it's also a good source of protein, and it's relatively low in calories, fat, and cholesterol.

Tuna's average protein content is about 24 grams per 3-ounce serving. That's a little more than you'd find in a cooked, 3-ounce hamburger.

Water-packed tuna has fewer calories than oil-packed. A water-packed brand has approximately 105 calories per half-can serving, compared with undrained oil-packed tuna's 240 calories per serving. However, if you prefer the taste of oil-packed tuna, drain the oil. This reduces the caloric difference between the two types to only 75.

Water-packed tuna averages 1.5 grams of fat per half-can serving. The average fat content of undrained, oil-packed tuna is about 16 grams—or 10 grams if the oil is drained off.

Excluding low-salt brands, tuna's sodium content is quite high—averaging 400 milligrams per half-can serving. (Draining an oil-packed brand should reduce its sodium content by about 15 percent.)

Tuna Varieties. According to the U.S. Food and Drug Administration, 12 different fish can be called tuna. But only one, albacore, can be labeled "white-meat" tuna.

White tuna has a light flesh and a characteristically mild flavor. Other tunas, such as yellowfin, bluefin, and skipjack, are darker, a bit more robust in flavor, and are labeled "light-meat" tuna. The delicate taste of white tuna isn't necessarily better than light tuna; it's a matter of personal preference. Both can be used interchangeably in many recipes.

Generally, white tuna comes in solid style and, less often, in chunk style. Light tuna comes most often in chunk, occasionally in solid style or—less expensively—in grated or flaked styles. The words *fancy* and *selected* simply tell you that the tuna is solid rather than chunk.

TURKEY

How a turkey tastes has to do with genetic factors, with feed, and with how it's raised. Small farmers often stock different breeds of birds and let them run free. A bird bought fresh-killed from a local farm should have a fresher, gamier taste than a bird that's been frozen or one that's spent some time in the supermarket chain of distribution.

How to Cook. To get the best out of the bird, cook a turkey uncovered, breast up, in a 325°F oven, until it reaches an internal temperature of 185°F. Using a meat thermometer is the most accurate way of telling when a turkey is done. Tugging gently on a bird's leg to see if it lifts easily away from the body is not always reliable. Neither is the pop-up thermometer included with many turkeys.

Some people try to make a turkey juicier by covering it and letting it cook in its own juices. But by doing this, they miss out on some of the complex flavors that come from roasting. To increase juiciness without drying out the bird, try basting, oiling the breast before roasting, or covering the breast with aluminum foil. You can also cut off the neck skin near the neck cavity and stretch it over the breast, securing it with toothpicks.

Calories. Like chicken, turkey is low in calories and saturated fat. People who are watching their fat intake may want to avoid dark meat, which is about twice as fatty as white meat.

However, even the dark meat is fairly lean compared with other meats. It's better to avoid eating the skin at all. Ounce for ounce, skin has about 12 times as much fat as white meat.

Additives. Most processors add a prebasting solution that is injected into the turkey in order to enhance juiciness. But the fats, salt, phosphates, flavoring, broth, and water that make up the solution don't really do very much. Fat, usually in the form of vegetable oil, is also added for flavor, but much of it ends up in the drip pan. Some turkey processors try to enhance flavor by adding sweeteners or monosodium glutamate (MSG). Some people have a negative reaction to MSG; if you are sensitive to it, check the ingredients list on the packaged turkey carefully before buying.

Food Poisoning. Take a few simple precautions when storing and preparing a turkey:

• A frozen turkey thaws faster than you think it will, particularly on a warm day or in a heated car. Go straight home and store the turkey in the refrigerator or freezer immediately.

• Wash your hands before and after handling the turkey. Wear gloves if you have cuts, abrasions, or skin infections.

• The safest way to thaw turkey (or any frozen food, for that matter) is in the refrigerator with a tray underneath to catch drips. An 8-pound bird will thaw in about a day; allow an extra day for every additional 4 pounds. For quick thawing, put the turkey in a watertight plastic bag, place the bagged bird in a large bowl or a clean sink, and cover it with *cold* water (to keep bacteria from multiplying on the outside of the bird while the inside thaws). Change the water every half hour. An 8-pound bird should thaw in about 4 hours; a 24-pound bird, in about 12 hours. If you have a microwave oven large enough to hold the turkey, use it for thawing, following the oven's instructions for power settings and thawing times.

- All raw poultry should be rinsed with cold water, to wash bacteria from the surface.
- After handling raw poultry, scrub your hands, utensils, and all work surfaces thoroughly. Chopping boards, butcher-block countertops, and other surfaces made of porous wood should be scrubbed with soap and hot water.
- You can't judge doneness by color. In young turkeys, for example, the bones are porous enough so that red color from the marrow occasionally seeps into the meat. When that happens, the legs and thighs look red and undercooked even after they are thoroughly cooked.
- Don't get too attached to turkey leftovers. Eat what you can in 2 or 3 days, then either freeze what's left or throw it away.

TURKEY ROLLS

Love turkey but hate to deal with it? Turkey rolls and roasts look appealing because of their easy preparation—no thawing, basting, stuffing, or disguising the leftovers. But they are not very good. These rolls can be gristly, salty, oily, wet instead of juicy, and may taste heavily of broth and processing—and usually they don't have much turkey flavor.

As far as nutrition goes, a serving of turkey roll has about the same number of calories as a serving of turkey breast. But the roll derives fewer of those calories from protein and more from fat. The rolls also contain a lot of sodium—about 600 milligrams in a 3.5-ounce serving. Turkey breast, by contrast, contains about one-third as much sodium.

Finally, turkey rolls are much more expensive, pound for pound, than whole turkeys.

Typewriters *(see Electronic Typewriters)*

VACUUM CLEANERS

Vacuum cleaners aren't interchangeable. The kind to buy depends on the jobs you want to do:

Uprights. An upright vacuum cleaner does the best job on carpets. Its power-driven, rotating beater/brush does most of the work; the suction serves mainly to blow the dirt into a filter bag on the handle. However, upright models aren't very useful for bare floors, and they're awkward in tight places. An upright can often be fitted with hoses and attachments to handle crevices and under-sofa or above-floor chores, but the arrangement is apt to be clumsy.

Canisters. A canister vacuum, with its higher suction, does the jobs an upright can't do well—bare floors, dusting, and the like. A canister is generally easy to use with attachments. However, an ordinary canister won't clean rugs as well as an upright. The canister relies on suction alone for cleaning; it picks up only surface dirt and debris, not deep-down grit.

Power-Nozzle Canisters. A canister with a power-nozzle attachment combines an upright's deep-cleaning ability with a canister's convenience and versatility. Unfortunately, it also retains some of the canister's drawbacks. Some assembly is always required, as is a good tug on the hose every now and then to keep the canister trailing along behind you.

Compact Canisters. You can generally carry a small version of a full-size canister in one hand while you clean with the other. Compacts are good in places where you can't take a full-size machine—the stairs or your car, for example. Some models have a power nozzle.

Lightweight Uprights. These look a bit like regular upright cleaners, but they lack a powered beater/brush. They're easy to handle and quite useful for quick cleanups of surface debris on carpets or bare floors.

VACUUM CLEANERS: CORDLESS

Like many other cordless devices, the mini-vacuum, or hand-held vacuum, owes its existence to the rechargeable battery. Aside from its charging stand, a cordless vacuum typically consists of two elements: a motor/handle combination that holds the battery, and a nozzle/collector unit that sucks up and stores the dirt. To empty most models, you simply push a release button, separate the parts, and shake out the collector.

When not in use, the vacuum cleaner belongs on its combination battery-charger/holder, which can be wall-mounted. Plugged into a wall outlet, a charger draws only a tiny amount of power—typically less than 5 watts.

In addition to doing a variety of odd jobs around the house, most cordless vacs are effective for regular cleanups of a reasonably tidy car. However, a full-size vacuum cleaner will do the job far better if the car is very dirty or if the debris is pebbly.

Don't ever use a cordless vacuum, unless it is a wet-dry model, on wet material or in a damp area such as a patio after rain; moisture could damage the machine.

VIDEOCASSETTE RECORDERS

Many people use their VCRs primarily for watching movies or for time-shifting—recording a program that they want to watch at a later time. If that's how you plan to use a VCR, get one that's easy to program and that can record all the shows you want within a certain time period. Every VCR lets you do some time-shifting; as models become more expensive, they generally offer greater time-shifting ability.

For playing prerecorded video tapes (and doing a minimum amount of time-shifting), the most basic VCR will do. However, if you are concerned about good-quality music reproduction, you should consider a higher-priced VCR that has hi-fi sound.

A lot of people now make their own video home movies using a camcorder (a camera with a built-in video recorder) that plays back through a VCR. To do this, you may want a fairly full-featured VCR with editing and sound-dubbing capability.

Cable TV. Most VCRs are "cable ready" in the sense that you can attach the cable to a connector on the back of the machine. True cable readiness means that the VCR can receive nonscrambled cable-TV channels directly, with no need for a cable-converter box or other hardware. The cable won't affect the VCR's time-shifting ability. You may, however, need a converter box to receive the so-called premium channels, such as HBO and Showtime.

Features. No matter which VCR you choose, look for these conveniences:

- a tuner that lets you bring in any available channel easily and that can receive all the channels that are in your area
- on-screen programming, which lets you set the VCR to record automatically with a minimum of fuss and frustration
- one-touch recording, which lets you start recording instantly

Don't assume that you will get a better picture by spending more money. By moving up in price, you will get a VCR with greater versatility, high-quality audio recording, and the ability to receive stereo TV sound. You have to go toward the middle of a manufacturer's line to get a VCR with tape-editing and dubbing features or a unit that can record a lot of programs.

VIDEOTAPES

If you buy standard-grade videotapes, you're doing the right thing. Manufacturers' grade designations don't help much in identifying the best tape. One company's "super-high" grade is often no better than another company's—or even its own— "high" grade. The performance of each brand's various grades is often indistinguishable. The overall quality of brand-name videotape is quite high, regardless of grade.

Gaps, scratches, or a poorly applied magnetic coating cause the intermittent flecks and streaks called dropouts. All video-cassette recorders have circuitry that replaces missing bits of picture lines with corresponding bits from the line above, a trick that ordinarily goes undetected by the viewer.

Sound. Until recently, all VCRs used the "linear-track" method to record sound; in this process, a narrow strip was reserved along the tape's edge for the sound track. However, the tape's low speed made good audio quality difficult to achieve.

A few years ago, high-fidelity sound was introduced in VCRs, using the tape's full width. In response, tape manufacturers introduced new tape grades with names that sound as though the tapes have been engineered especially for hi-fi VCRs. In fact, almost any brand-name tape should give excellent audio results with any hi-fi VCR.

Licensed Tapes. The JVC and Sony companies, originators of the VHS and Beta tape formats, respectively, license other manufacturers to produce videotape. These tapes carry an official VHS or Beta logo. Before buying an unfamiliar tape brand, check the packaging to see if the tape is licensed. Unlicensed tape may tend to have defects—excessive drop-outs, considerable noise, and the like.

Some unlicensed tapes avoid using an official logo. Others skirt the legal edge by using the logo in a sentence rather than having it stand alone. Another tip-off is the absence of an address for the manufacturer or distributor.

VITAMIN SUPPLEMENTS

It's possible to overdose on some vitamins. Fat-soluble vitamins are not excreted efficiently—generally stored in the body until used up, they can accumulate to toxic levels. For example, prolonged excessive intake of vitamin A can cause headache, increased pressure on the brain, bone pain, and damage to the liver. Excessive vitamin-D dosage can cause high blood calcium levels and kidney damage.

Though the water-soluble vitamins are generally excreted quickly when taken to excess, some of them can cause trouble. Large doses of niacin can cause severe flushes, skin rash, and abnormal liver-function tests. High doses of vitamin C can cause diarrhea. And high doses of vitamin B_6 over long periods can cause permanent damage to the peripheral nervous system.

The best way to get vitamins is from foods found in a balanced diet. Vitamin supplementation may be appropriate for children up to 2 years old, children who have poor eating habits, some people on prolonged weight-reduction programs, pregnant women, strict vegetarians (those who avoid eggs and milk as well as meat), and for sick people as directed by a physician.

Rather than take vitamins for "insurance," evaluate your diet to determine whether you are eating a variety of foods from the Basic Four groups. If you have trouble figuring this out by yourself, record what you eat for a week and ask a registered dietician or a physician whether you are missing anything. If you are, the best course of action will probably be to improve your eating habits, not to supplement your diet with vitamins.

As a rule, don't take more than the RDA amounts (the Recommended Dietary Allowances published by the Food and Nutrition Board of the National Research Council/National Academy of Sciences), and avoid doctors or nutrition consultants who recommend vitamins as cure-alls.

Minerals. A fair number of Americans may need more of certain minerals than they get from their diets. Here are three minerals that warrant special attention:

Fluoride intake throughout childhood helps build decay-resistant teeth. The most efficient, economical way to get it is through fluoridated water. Children who grow up in non-fluoridated communities should take supplemental fluoride (by prescription) from birth through age 12.

Calcium deserves particular attention because inadequate calcium intake is a factor in the development of osteoporosis, or thinning of the bones, especially in women. Those who like milk, cheese, and other dairy products may get what they need from diet alone (*see* Calcium and Nutrition). But those consuming little calcium-rich food should seek advice on supplementation from a doctor or registered dietician.

Iron is needed to make hemoglobin, the component in red blood cells that carries oxygen to the tissues. Lack of sufficient iron causes iron-deficiency anemia. Women who are pregnant or who menstruate heavily should be checked by a doctor to be sure they are not anemic.

WAFFLE MAKERS

A waffle maker isn't a necessity. There are always pancakes or frozen waffles. But if you would rather go without than eat a frozen waffle, or if you think Saturdays or Sundays are meant for lavish breakfasts, a waffle maker could be one of life's small luxuries.

Waffle lovers would do well to choose a product that offers a choice of browning levels and a signal light to tell when the waffles are cooked to the desired degree.

Consumers also have the choice of buying either a traditional waffle maker or one that comes with a multipurpose grid for grilling sandwiches and hamburgers and for baking wafer cookies known as pizzelles. Generally, the absence of a grill or pizzelle maker isn't very important. No one who owns a range and frying pan really needs a grill.

The waffle-cooking grids on today's waffle makers have nonstick coatings. As long as they are oiled lightly before each fresh use, there should not be any serious sticking problems. The removable grids found on some waffle makers have a decided advantage if you want to wash away excess oil: They can be dunked in warm, sudsy water.

Safety Tips. The plastic handle used to open and close a waffle maker's lid during cooking should be large enough to provide a good grip, so that your fingers won't touch a surface that can reach nearly 300°F. The handle should also be designed to shield fingers from escaping steam.

WALKABOUT STEREO PLAYERS

If you want to have music wherever you go, most lightweight, compact, portable tape players are capable of delivering good sound quality. Unfortunately, a good deal of that performance potential goes to waste when you actually walk about with a player. A walkabout's headphones generally don't deliver a wide range of sound. But this doesn't mean the sound will be unpleasant—even mediocre headphones create a "super-stereo" effect that can draw your attention away from any defects in the sound.

Furthermore, moving around with a walkabout may increase tape flutter—an unpleasant wavering of the sound caused by fluctuations in tape speed. A unit with a snug belt clip is likely to jiggle the least and so produce the least flutter.

A built-in radio may also not work as well as you would like. A walkabout uses the headphone wire as the radio antenna; moving around may cause the program (especially FM stereo) to fade in and out, because the antenna is shifting in relation to the station's transmitter. Even when you're sitting down, you may have to adjust the wire for the best reception.

Convenience. Most walkabouts come with a handy clip that slips over a belt. A walkabout with a shoulder strap may jiggle around too much. A unit with a belt loop rather than a clip forces you to unbuckle your belt to strap it on.

Control Position. It's best to have the tape and tuner controls on top so you can look down on them when the unit is clipped to your belt.

Tape Controls. A number of units reverse automatically when they reach the end of a tape. Other handy tape features include a light to tell you the tape is running, which helps to remind you to turn off the player when you take off the headphones. An automatic stop after rewind not only means one less button to press, but it also helps conserve the batteries.

Tone and Volume Controls. An equalizer lets you adjust different bands of the music spectrum. However, an equalizer doesn't have much of an edge over conventional tone controls.

Tape-Head Cleaning. The tape head should be at the hinge side of the tape hatch. This makes it easy to reach the heads for cleaning.

Loudness. It's possible to play some walkabouts loud enough and long enough to endanger your hearing. Most people turn down the volume before it becomes painfully loud. Nevertheless, a person could learn to live with the volume turned up—especially if the music is blocking out some other loud ambient noise, such as a lawn mower.

You should think twice about jogging, cycling, or driving with a walkabout playing loud enough to drown out car horns or sirens. In many communities it's against the law to wear headphones if you're behind the wheel or jogging down the road.

Warranties *(see Automobile Warranties)*

WASHING MACHINES

The real trend in washing machines over the past 25 years has been toward sameness, not innovation. Today, just about any machine you buy will be able to wash a load of clothes satisfactorily. The chief differences these days are in available features.

Controls. Dials and levers are adequate, cheaper to service, and often more versatile than the touch-pad controls commonly found on more expensive models.

Wash Cycle. In all automatic machines, this cycle consists of wash-spin-rinse-spin. Full-featured machines generally have at least three such cycles, for regular, permanent-press, and delicate fabrics. Some have an extra cycle for soak or prewash.

The permanent-press cycle is generally a few minutes shorter than the regular cycle. It helps prevent setting wrinkles in two ways. First, clothes are cooled down with a cold spray or cold rinse before the first spin cycle. Then, the spin speed itself is slower so clothes don't become so compressed. This leaves them a bit wetter than regular wash at the end of the cycle.

The delicate cycle has slower agitation and spin than the regular wash cycle.

Speed Control. A selector for wash and spin is often built into the cycle control, but sometimes you have to set speeds independently.

Water-level Control. The less hot water you use, the cheaper it is to run the machine. A level control lets you adjust the amount of water to the size of the wash load, thereby saving water, detergent, and energy.

Temperature Setting. Any machine can give you either hot or cold water as it comes from the pipes, or warm, which is about a half-and-half mix. In deciding which temperature setting to use, one consideration should be the type of fabric and its colorfastness. However, given the effectiveness of good modern detergents, there's another consideration: since you can save about half of your water-heating cost by using a warm wash instead of hot, there's really little reason to use the hot setting at all—except for the occasional wash that will only come clean with the hottest water available.

Always use a cold rinse. Warm water doesn't rinse clothes any better.

Tub Capacity. A large tub is desirable because it is more efficient, making it possible to do a few large loads rather than many small ones.

Additional Cycles. In addition to the basic cycles, alternate washing cycles may be available, depending on how deluxe a machine you decide to buy. *Soak/prewash* is for heavily soiled clothes. *Extra rinse* gives you two rinses instead of one. *Sequential* means you can let the extra cycle proceed automatically; otherwise, the machine stops before or afterward, and you set the next step yourself. An *automatic bleach dispenser* adds bleach to the wash water after water has filled the tub. A *timed bleach dispenser* adds the bleach to the water toward the end of the wash cycle so that the brighteners in the detergent can work better. A *softener dispenser* holds fabric softener and dispenses it during the rinse cycle so it won't conflict with the detergent.

Within a manufacturer's line of washing machines, a number of models often share the principal mechanical parts and so should perform similarly. If you decide to buy a less expensive washer, in most cases all you give up are presoak and extra-rinse cycles and automatic dispensers for bleach and fabric softener.

Front-loading Washers. Americans usually prefer top-loading washing machines, which have a larger capacity and don't make you squat to load and unload. However, a front-loading machine has two distinct advantages: you can stack a full-sized dryer above it, and it uses less water and energy than a top loader.

WATER
Excellent water, still or sparkling, should taste fresh and clean. After you swallow, it should leave your mouth refreshed. It should be clear and free of sediment, with no aroma whatsoever and no hint of any chemical taste such as chlorine. But the taste of excellent water isn't exactly no taste at all. Flatness—a lifeless taste—is a defect, often the result of very low mineral content.

Tap water shouldn't be brown, cloudy, or murky-looking.

It shouldn't foam or have a discernible odor. And there shouldn't be sudden changes in the water's appearance, taste, or aroma.

Many toxic hazards found in water are invisible, tasteless, and odorless. Laboratory analysis is the only sure way to confirm that water meets safety standards. If you are concerned about the quality of your drinking water, the U.S. Environmental Protection Agency (EPA) suggests you first try contacting your local water or health department. They may check and test your tap water at no charge. But it may be necessary for you to work your way up to your state's water-supply or health department.

Many times such agencies will test only for bacteria, not for toxic substances. So you might consider paying a commercial laboratory for such testing. One such lab is the WaterTest Corporation (PO Box 6360, 33 S. Commercial St., Manchester, NH 03108; 800-H2O-TEST). This company charges from $99.95 to $150, depending on how many aspects of the water you want tested. The lower-priced test covers 25 metals and minerals.

Improving Your Water. You can improve the taste, if not the quality, of your tap water in various ways. Boiling water for 20 minutes is the standard remedy for bacterial contamination, but that doesn't improve the taste, to say the least. Refrigerating water may well improve flavor, since heavy chlorine tastes and odors will dissipate if water is kept for several hours in an uncovered pitcher. Some people even suggest using a blender or mixer for several minutes to aerate water and remove chlorine and other volatile chemicals more efficiently. Or a simple faucet aerator may make flat-tasting water more palatable.

Home water-treatment systems are also available. They include activated carbon filters, some of which attach directly to the faucet or hook into the cold-water line under a sink.

Such filters can improve the taste and odor of water and can be highly effective in removing many organic chemicals. However, you must periodically replace the filter cartridges or you might actually wind up *adding* pollutants to the water. And a carbon filter won't remove toxic metals or excessive minerals.

Other home-treatment systems use reverse osmosis, ion-exchange resins, or distillation to soften water by removing minerals. The ion-exchange systems usually replace minerals with sodium, which can be undesirable for those who are restricting their dietary intake of sodium.

Water Varieties. Bottled water may come from a spring, a spa, a well, even a geyser. Or it may come from a public water supply. There's no government rule that obligates a company to disclose the location of its water source, though many brands do. The product, however, must accurately list the *type* of source on its label.

Spring water rises naturally to the earth's surface from reservoir-like water deposits in underground geological formations. Spring water emerges under its own pressure without any pumping required, though sometimes its flow is aided by a shallow pipe. Some companies that use the word *spring* in their brand name don't necessarily sell spring water. The bottle may be partly filtered well water.

Artesian water also bubbles up under its own pressure, though a well must be drilled to get at the water. The term *natural* may apply to well, spring, or other water sources. It means simply that the water's mineral content has not been altered. Natural water, though, may be filtered or otherwise treated.

Drinking water usually refers to well water that's been demineralized and then has had some minerals restored.

Distilled water and *purified water* are virtually free of minerals. Two states, California and Florida, have their own standard specifying how mineralized a water must be to be called "mineral water": at least 500 parts per million of dissolved solids. (If you imagine $\frac{1}{30}$ teaspoon of sugar dissolved in a bathtub of water, that's about 1 part per million.)

The difference between *club soda* and *seltzer* is mineral content. Club-soda manufacturers add mineral salts—bicarbonates, citrates, and phosphates of sodium, for instance. Seltzers have a much lower mineral content.

WOOD FINISHES: CLEAR

A clear finish—lacquer, varnish, or oil—seals wood without hiding the natural beauty of the wood grain.

Varnish. Varnish is essentially paint without pigment—a blend of oils and resins that coats the surface of the wood. The polyurethane so widely used on floors is just one type of oil-based varnish. Water-based varnishes, which clean up with water, are also available. Whatever the variety, varnish comes in high-, medium-, or low-gloss finish; you can even get varnish "stain," which is tinted to approximate certain wood tones.

Lacquer. Lacquer is a cellulose derivative that's been dissolved in strong solvents. As the solvents evaporate, the lacquer dries to form a thin, tough film. Most wood furniture sold today is finished with lacquer.

Penetrating Oil. Penetrating oil protects wood by soaking into its pores. It doesn't leave a surface coating, as varnish and lacquer do. As a result, oil doesn't do much to protect the wood from abrasion—the scuff of shoes on a floor or the scrape of dishes on a tabletop. However, oil gives wood a low luster that many people like. And because the oil doesn't cover the wood, you can feel the texture of the wood grain itself.

Application. Varnish and lacquer require a slightly different brushing technique than paint. As thin liquids, they tend to run and sag when applied. This is a particular problem if you're refinishing an ornate piece of furniture and every curve and curlicue becomes a trap for a drippy blob of finish.

Overall, varnishes are the easiest type to apply, especially the ones with latex formulations.

Lacquers are difficult to brush on. The first coat flows on easily; the second coat is another matter. It's the nature of lacquer that the fresh coat dissolves the previous one, impeding the flow and making the brush drag.

Penetrating oil isn't very difficult to apply, but it is messy and time-consuming.

Safety. Clear wood finishes have component materials that are flammable or dangerous to inhale. This problem is especially acute if you are refinishing a large area, such as a floor. Read and heed the instructions and safety warnings on the container.

Keep the work area well ventilated. Wear suitable clothing: a long-sleeved shirt and rubber gloves. Before you start, turn off any gas flames, including pilot lights—even those in neighboring rooms or down a flight of stairs. Don't smoke and don't use electrical equipment or other tools or appliances that could produce a spark or a flame.

Stirring. Do-it-yourself books often tell you not to stir varnish or lacquer; doing so creates bubbles that can show up on the finish as pockmarks or blisters. Nevertheless, some gentle stirring is usually necessary, especially with semigloss and satin varnish. The ingredients that give these finishes their lower gloss tend to settle to the bottom of the can, especially if the can has been sitting on a shelf for a long time. If you don't stir the varnish, you can wind up with a finish that's glossier than you want.

How to Apply. The best application method is to use several thin coats. Although these finishes are thin to begin with, you can usually thin them further, unless the label states otherwise. If you try to do the job with only one or two heavier coats, there may be sagging, wrinkling, or missed spots.

With varnish or lacquer, keep the brush full of finish. Don't work the brush back and forth, as you would with paint. Keep the finish and brush as wet as possible. If you miss a spot, don't backtrack to catch it; use the next coat to cover it.

Buy the best brush you can reasonably afford; brush quality is important with varnishes. Work in bright light; reflected light from the wet surface can help you spot missed areas. With small pieces, keep the work surface as horizontal as possible.

Sanding between coats is a must—if your eyes tell you otherwise, let your fingertips be the judge. Use the finest sandpaper your patience allows, or fine steel wool. Sand with the grain and be sure to get rid of all sanding dust before you apply the next coat.

Recommendations. A satin or semigloss varnish offers a compromise between a high-gloss varnish and a penetrating oil. The semigloss products are generally tougher than their high-gloss counterparts, and they come close to providing the natural-wood look of penetrating oils.

If you want a clear finish for a bookcase, coffee table, or the like, drying time and hardness are less important than resistance to blocking, the tendency to be just a bit sticky, even after the finish has had time to dry completely. Satin and semigloss varnishes and penetrating oils are good bets here.

WOOD STOVES

A cheery wood stove can be a quick, easy, and relatively inexpensive way to lower winter heating bills. A modern wood stove, especially one with a catalytic converter, burns cleaner than its predecessors and so contributes fewer pollutants to the air and less creosote up the chimney. It also burns more efficiently and so consumes less wood. Still, there are drawbacks to its use.

Cost. Any wood stove, old or new, is fundamentally an auxiliary heater. While a stove may cost much less to run than an electric heater, it costs considerably more to buy and install. A stove also requires much more of your time and attention than an electric heater.

You may not *need* a wood stove in order to cut your yearly heating costs. But you may decide you *want* a stove as much for its cheeriness as for its warmth.

In buying, you might want to choose among available models on the basis of price, installation dimensions, or a feature such as a window or an ash drawer.

Safety. Whatever stove you buy, be extremely careful about its installation. Don't do the work yourself unless you're an accomplished do-it-yourselfer. Check with the fire department or the local building inspector to find out what minimum clearances are required in your area and what materials are recommended or required as heat-shielding. Don't cut corners or skimp on materials. If you have a professional handle the installation, hire the company that has the best reputation and not necessarily the best price.

YOGURT AND HEALTH

Yogurt is the snack or lunch of choice for many dieters. Yet yogurt is a full-fledged relative of milk and butter. Whether regular or low-fat, it contains the same type of saturated fat that they do. Ounce for ounce, regular yogurt has approximately the same fat content as whole milk—roughly 3 percent. Low-fat yogurt, at about 2 percent fat, isn't much of an improvement over ordinary yogurt if you're trying to lower your blood cholesterol. Some medical advisers do not recommend either as standard fare for people who must watch their fat and cholesterol intake.

Yogurt made from skim milk, which contains less than 0.5 percent fat, is a better choice.

Index